Ancient Texts and the Bible
Book 9 - Easy Reader Edition

Israel...
Through the Book of Numbers

Minister 2 Others

Ancient Texts and the Bible
Book 9

Israel...
Through the Book of Numbers

Easy Reader Edition

Israel... Through the Book of Numbers
ISBN 978-1-947751-27-9

Ancient texts compiled for this series:

The Bible
King James Version 1769

The Book of Enoch
An English translation by Dr. Laurence,
Archbishop of Cashel,
Formerly Professor of Hebrew at Oxford, 1833

The Book of Jasher
Faithfully translated 1840
from the original Hebrew into English
Published by J.H. Parry & Company 1887

The Book of Jubileees
by R.H. Charles, Oxford: Clarendon Press, 1913

Ancient Texts and the Bible
series include:

Book 1: In The Beginning... From Adam to Noah

Book 2: In The Beginning... From Noah to Abraham

Book 3: In The Beginning... From Abraham to Israel

Book 4: In The Beginning... From Israel to Egypt

Book 5: In The Beginning... From Egypt to Goshen

Book 6: Israel... From Goshen to Sinai

Book 7: Israel... From Sinai to the Tabernacle

Book 8: Israel... Through the Book of Leviticus

Book 9: Israel... Through the Book of Numbers

Book 10: Israel... Through the Book of Joshua

Table of Contents:

Forward

The **Ancient Texts and the Bible** series synchronizes the manuscripts of Enoch, Jasher, and Jubileees into the Bible, making one complete storyline. The books are interwoven using the Torah as the backbone, and the extra-biblical texts as the fleshing out of that backbone.

The nineth book in the series contains the entire book of Numbers, as well as the book of Jasher chapters 83 through 86.

Though the language in the writings have been updated, replacing words like "*thou*" and "*thine*" with words like "*you*" and "*your*", the integrity of the verses remain.

The "*Easy Reader*" edition is for those who just want to read the storyline and enjoy the journey. The stop signs and complex formatting have been removed so one may merely focus upon the story being told.

The *Expanded Edition* of **Ancient Texts and the Bible** was created for the more studious reader. The various manuscripts have the following formatting applied to them in this edition:

the Bible - Regular

THE BOOK OF ENOCH - ALL CAPITALS

the Book of Jasher - Italics

<u>the Book of Jubileees - Underlined</u>

Where one of the extra-biblical texts reiterates the Bible, the phrase is then put in a **bold font**. Where two manuscripts overlap each other exclusive of the Bible, then both fonts are used. For instance, where Jasher and Jubileees intercept, the text is then formatted as *Italics and Underlined*.

The stop sign is another element to the *Expanded Edition* that is not seen in the *Easy Reader*. This image points to contradictions in the content. Printed versions also contain page numbers within the stop sign revealing the page where contradictory information is located, and vice versa. This information was not feasible to place in the e-book versions since the page numbers vary depending on the font size the reader chooses. Following, is an example from each edition:

Easy Reader Edition:

(Numbers 1:2) (Jasher 83:18...)
Take you the sum of all the heads of the congregation of the children of Israel, after their families, by the house of their fathers, with the number of their names, every male by their polls;

Expanded Edition:

(Numbers 1:2) (Jasher 83:18...)
Take you the sum of all *the heads of* the congregation of **the children of Israel,** after their families, by the house of their fathers, with the number of their names, **every male** by their polls;

Whichever you choose, may you ***Enjoy the Journey***!

Numbers: Chapter One

(Numbers 1:1) (Jasher 83:17)
And the LORD spoke to Moses in the wilderness of Sinai, in the tabernacle of the congregation, on the first day of the second month, in the second year after they were come out of the land of Egypt, saying,

(Numbers 1:2) (Jasher 83:18...)
Take you the sum of all the heads of the congregation of the children of Israel, after their families, by the house of their fathers, with the number of their names, every male by their polls;

(Numbers 1:3) (...Jasher 83:18...)
From twenty years old and upward, all that are able to go forth to war in Israel: you and your brother Aaron shall number them by their armies.

(Numbers 1:4)
And with you there shall be a man of every tribe; every one head of the house of his fathers.

(Numbers 1:5)
And these are the names of the men that shall stand with you: of the tribe of Reuben; Elizur the son of Shedeur.

(Numbers 1:6)
Of Simeon; Shelumiel the son of Zurishaddai.

(Numbers 1:7)
Of Judah; Nahshon the son of Amminadab.

(Numbers 1:8)
Of Issachar; Nethaneel the son of Zuar.

(Numbers 1:9)
Of Zebulun; Eliab the son of Helon.

(Numbers 1:10)
Of the children of Joseph: of Ephraim; Elishama the son of Ammihud: of Manasseh; Gamaliel the son of Pedahzur.

(Numbers 1:11)
Of Benjamin; Abidan the son of Gideoni.

(Numbers 1:12)
Of Dan; Ahiezer the son of Ammishaddai.

(Numbers 1:13)
Of Asher; Pagiel the son of Ocran.

(Numbers 1:14)
Of Gad; Eliasaph the son of Deuel.

(Numbers 1:15)
Of Naphtali; Ahira the son of Enan.

(Numbers 1:16) (...Jasher 83:18)
These were the renowned of the congregation, twelve princes of the tribes of their fathers of Israel, heads of thousands in Israel.

(Numbers 1:17)
And Moses and Aaron took these men which are expressed by their names:

(Numbers 1:18)

And they assembled all the congregation together on the first day of the second month, and they declared their pedigrees after their families, by the house of their fathers, according to the number of the names, from twenty years old and upward, by their polls.

(Numbers 1:19) (Jasher 83:19)

As the LORD commanded Moses, Moses did so, and Aaron came with the twelve princes of Israel, so he numbered them in the wilderness of Sinai.

(Numbers 1:20)

And the children of Reuben, Israel's eldest son, by their generations, after their families, by the house of their fathers, according to the number of the names, by their polls, every male from twenty years old and upward, all that were able to go forth to war;

(Numbers 1:21)

Those that were numbered of them, even of the tribe of Reuben, were forty and six thousand and five hundred.

(Numbers 1:22)

Of the children of Simeon, by their generations, after their families, by the house of their fathers, those that were numbered of them, according to the number of the names, by their polls, every male from twenty years old and upward, all that were able to go forth to war;

(Numbers 1:23)

Those that were numbered of them, even of the tribe of Simeon, were fifty and nine thousand and three hundred.

(Numbers 1:24)

Of the children of Gad, by their generations, after their families, by the house of their fathers, according to the number of the names, from twenty years old and upward, all that were able to go forth to war;

(Numbers 1:25)

Those that were numbered of them, even of the tribe of Gad, were forty and five thousand six hundred and fifty.

(Numbers 1:26)

Of the children of Judah, by their generations, after their families, by the house of their fathers, according to the number of the names, from twenty years old and upward, all that were able to go forth to war;

(Numbers 1:27)

Those that were numbered of them, even of the tribe of Judah, were threescore and fourteen thousand and six hundred.

(Numbers 1:28)

Of the children of Issachar, by their generations, after their families, by the house of their fathers, according to the number of the names, from twenty years old and upward, all that were able to go forth to war;

(Numbers 1:29)

Those that were numbered of them, even of the tribe of Issachar, were fifty and four thousand and four hundred.

(Numbers 1:30)

Of the children of Zebulun, by their generations, after their families, by the house of their fathers, according to the number of the names, from twenty years old and upward, all that were able to go forth to war;

(Numbers 1:31)
Those that were numbered of them, even of the tribe of Zebulun, were fifty and seven thousand and four hundred.

(Numbers 1:32)
Of the children of Joseph, namely, of the children of Ephraim, by their generations, after their families, by the house of their fathers, according to the number of the names, from twenty years old and upward, all that were able to go forth to war;

(Numbers 1:33)
Those that were numbered of them, even of the tribe of Ephraim, were forty thousand and five hundred.

(Numbers 1:34)
Of the children of Manasseh, by their generations, after their families, by the house of their fathers, according to the number of the names, from twenty years old and upward, all that were able to go forth to war;

(Numbers 1:35)
Those that were numbered of them, even of the tribe of Manasseh, were thirty and two thousand and two hundred.

(Numbers 1:36)
Of the children of Benjamin, by their generations, after their families, by the house of their fathers, according to the number of the names, from twenty years old and upward, all that were able to go forth to war;

(Numbers 1:37)
Those that were numbered of them, even of the tribe of

Benjamin, were thirty and five thousand and four hundred.

(Numbers 1:38)
Of the children of Dan, by their generations, after their families, by the house of their fathers, according to the number of the names, from twenty years old and upward, all that were able to go forth to war;

(Numbers 1:39)
Those that were numbered of them, even of the tribe of Dan, were threescore and two thousand and seven hundred.

(Numbers 1:40)
Of the children of Asher, by their generations, after their families, by the house of their fathers, according to the number of the names, from twenty years old and upward, all that were able to go forth to war;

(Numbers 1:41)
Those that were numbered of them, even of the tribe of Asher, were forty and one thousand and five hundred.

(Numbers 1:42)
Of the children of Naphtali, throughout their generations, after their families, by the house of their fathers, according to the number of the names, from twenty years old and upward, all that were able to go forth to war;

(Numbers 1:43)
Those that were numbered of them, even of the tribe of Naphtali, were fifty and three thousand and four hundred.

(Numbers 1:44)
These are those that were numbered, which Moses and Aaron

numbered, and the princes of Israel, being twelve men: each one was for the house of his fathers.

(Numbers 1:45) (Jasher 83:20...)
So were all those that were numbered of the children of Israel, by the house of their fathers, from twenty years old and upward, all that were able to go forth to war in Israel;

(Numbers 1:46) (...Jasher 83:20)
Even all they that were numbered were six hundred thousand and three thousand and five hundred and fifty.

(Numbers 1:47) (Jasher 83:21)
But the Levites after the tribe of their fathers were not numbered among them.

(Jasher 83:22)
And the number of all the males of the children of Israel from one month old and upward, was twenty-two thousand, two hundred and seventy-three.

(Jasher 83:23)
And the number of the children of Levi from one month old and above, was twenty-two thousand.

(Numbers 1:48)
For the LORD had spoken to Moses, saying,

(Numbers 1:49)
Only you shall not number the tribe of Levi, neither take the sum of them among the children of Israel:

(Numbers 1:50)
But you shall appoint the Levites over the tabernacle of

testimony, and over all the vessels thereof, and over all things that belong to it: they shall bear the tabernacle, and all the vessels thereof; and they shall minister to it, and shall encamp round about the tabernacle.

(Numbers 1:51)
And when the tabernacle sets forward, the Levites shall take it down: and when the tabernacle is to be pitched, the Levites shall set it up: and the stranger that comes nigh shall be put to death.

(Jasher 83:24)
And Moses placed the priests and the Levites each man to his service and to his burden to serve the sanctuary of the tabernacle, as the Lord had commanded Moses.

(Numbers 1:52)
And the children of Israel shall pitch their tents, every man by his own camp, and every man by his own standard, throughout their hosts.

(Numbers 1:53)
But the Levites shall pitch round about the tabernacle of testimony, that there be no wrath upon the congregation of the children of Israel: and the Levites shall keep the charge of the tabernacle of testimony.

(Numbers 1:54)
And the children of Israel did according to all that the LORD commanded Moses, so did they.

Numbers: Chapter Two

(Numbers 2:1)
And the LORD spoke to Moses and to Aaron, saying,

(Numbers 2:2)
Every man of the children of Israel shall pitch by his own standard, with the ensign of their father's house: far off about the tabernacle of the congregation shall they pitch.

(Numbers 2:3)
And on the east side toward the rising of the sun shall they of the standard of the camp of Judah pitch throughout their armies: and Nahshon the son of Amminadab shall be captain of the children of Judah.

(Numbers 2:4)
And his host, and those that were numbered of them, were threescore and fourteen thousand and six hundred.

(Numbers 2:5)
And those that do pitch next to him shall be the tribe of Issachar: and Nethaneel the son of Zuar shall be captain of the children of Issachar.

(Numbers 2:6)
And his host, and those that were numbered thereof, were fifty and four thousand and four hundred.

(Numbers 2:7)
Then the tribe of Zebulun: and Eliab the son of Helon shall be

captain of the children of Zebulun.

(Numbers 2:8)

And his host, and those that were numbered thereof, were fifty and seven thousand and four hundred.

(Numbers 2:9)

All that were numbered in the camp of Judah were an hundred thousand and fourscore thousand and six thousand and four hundred, throughout their armies. These shall first set forth.

(Numbers 2:10)

On the south side shall be the standard of the camp of Reuben according to their armies: and the captain of the children of Reuben shall be Elizur the son of Shedeur.

(Numbers 2:11)

And his host, and those that were numbered thereof, were forty and six thousand and five hundred.

(Numbers 2:12)

And those which pitch by him shall be the tribe of Simeon: and the captain of the children of Simeon shall be Shelumiel the son of Zurishaddai.

(Numbers 2:13)

And his host, and those that were numbered of them, were fifty and nine thousand and three hundred.

(Numbers 2:14)

Then the tribe of Gad: and the captain of the sons of Gad shall be Eliasaph the son of Reuel.

(Numbers 2:15)

And his host, and those that were numbered of them, were forty and five thousand and six hundred and fifty.

(Numbers 2:16)

All that were numbered in the camp of Reuben were an hundred thousand and fifty and one thousand and four hundred and fifty, throughout their armies. And they shall set forth in the second rank.

(Numbers 2:17)

Then the tabernacle of the congregation shall set forward with the camp of the Levites in the midst of the camp: as they encamp, so shall they set forward, every man in his place by their standards.

(Numbers 2:18)

On the west side shall be the standard of the camp of Ephraim according to their armies: and the captain of the sons of Ephraim shall be Elishama the son of Ammihud.

(Numbers 2:19)

And his host, and those that were numbered of them, were forty thousand and five hundred.

(Numbers 2:20)

And by him shall be the tribe of Manasseh: and the captain of the children of Manasseh shall be Gamaliel the son of Pedahzur.

(Numbers 2:21)

And his host, and those that were numbered of them, were thirty and two thousand and two hundred.

(Numbers 2:22)
Then the tribe of Benjamin: and the captain of the sons of Benjamin shall be Abidan the son of Gideoni.

(Numbers 2:23)
And his host, and those that were numbered of them, were thirty and five thousand and four hundred.

(Numbers 2:24)
All that were numbered of the camp of Ephraim were an hundred thousand and eight thousand and an hundred, throughout their armies. And they shall go forward in the third rank.

(Numbers 2:25)
The standard of the camp of Dan shall be on the north side by their armies: and the captain of the children of Dan shall be Ahiezer the son of Ammishaddai.

(Numbers 2:26)
And his host, and those that were numbered of them, were threescore and two thousand and seven hundred.

(Numbers 2:27)
And those that encamp by him shall be the tribe of Asher: and the captain of the children of Asher shall be Pagiel the son of Ocran.

(Numbers 2:28)
And his host, and those that were numbered of them, were forty and one thousand and five hundred.

(Numbers 2:29)
Then the tribe of Naphtali: and the captain of the children of

Naphtali shall be Ahira the son of Enan.

(Numbers 2:30)

And his host, and those that were numbered of them, were fifty and three thousand and four hundred.

(Numbers 2:31)

All they that were numbered in the camp of Dan were an hundred thousand and fifty and seven thousand and six hundred. They shall go hindmost with their standards.

(Numbers 2:32)

These are those which were numbered of the children of Israel by the house of their fathers: all those that were numbered of the camps throughout their hosts were six hundred thousand and three thousand and five hundred and fifty.

(Numbers 2:33)

But the Levites were not numbered among the children of Israel; as the LORD commanded Moses.

(Numbers 2:34)

And the children of Israel did according to all that the LORD commanded Moses: so they pitched by their standards, and so they set forward, every one after their families, according to the house of their fathers.

Numbers: Chapter Three

(Numbers 3:1)
These also are the generations of Aaron and Moses in the day that the LORD spoke with Moses in mount Sinai.

(Numbers 3:2)
And these are the names of the sons of Aaron; Nadab the firstborn, and Abihu, Eleazar, and Ithamar.

(Numbers 3:3)
These are the names of the sons of Aaron, the priests which were anointed, whom he consecrated to minister in the priest's office.

(Numbers 3:4)
And Nadab and Abihu died before the LORD, when they offered strange fire before the LORD, in the wilderness of Sinai, and they had no children: and Eleazar and Ithamar ministered in the priest's office in the sight of Aaron their father.

(Numbers 3:5)
And the LORD spoke to Moses, saying,

(Numbers 3:6)
Bring the tribe of Levi near, and present them before Aaron the priest, that they may minister to him.

(Numbers 3:7)
And they shall keep his charge, and the charge of the whole

congregation before the tabernacle of the congregation, to do the service of the tabernacle.

(Numbers 3:8)

And they shall keep all the instruments of the tabernacle of the congregation, and the charge of the children of Israel, to do the service of the tabernacle.

(Numbers 3:9)

And you shall give the Levites to Aaron and to his sons: they are wholly given to him out of the children of Israel.

(Numbers 3:10)

And you shall appoint Aaron and his sons, and they shall wait on their priest's office: and the stranger that comes nigh shall be put to death.

(Numbers 3:11)

And the LORD spoke to Moses, saying,

(Numbers 3:12)

And I, behold, I have taken the Levites from among the children of Israel instead of all the firstborn that opens the matrix among the children of Israel: therefore the Levites shall be mine;

(Numbers 3:13)

Because all the firstborn are mine; for on the day that I smote all the firstborn in the land of Egypt I hallowed to me all the firstborn in Israel, both man and beast: mine shall they are: I am the LORD.

(Numbers 3:14)
And the LORD spoke to Moses in the wilderness of Sinai, saying,

(Numbers 3:15)
Number the children of Levi after the house of their fathers, by their families: every male from a month old and upward shall you number them.

(Numbers 3:16)
And Moses numbered them according to the word of the LORD, as he was commanded.

(Numbers 3:17)
And these were the sons of Levi by their names; Gershon, and Kohath, and Merari.

(Numbers 3:18)
And these are the names of the sons of Gershon by their families; Libni, and Shimei.

(Numbers 3:19)
And the sons of Kohath by their families; Amram, and Izehar, Hebron, and Uzziel.

(Numbers 3:20)
And the sons of Merari by their families; Mahli, and Mushi. These are the families of the Levites according to the house of their fathers.

(Numbers 3:21)
Of Gershon was the family of the Libnites, and the family of the Shimites: these are the families of the Gershonites.

(Numbers 3:22)
Those that were numbered of them, according to the number of all the males, from a month old and upward, even those that were numbered of them were seven thousand and five hundred.

(Numbers 3:23)
The families of the Gershonites shall pitch behind the tabernacle westward.

(Numbers 3:24)
And the chief of the house of the father of the Gershonites shall be Eliasaph the son of Lael.

(Numbers 3:25)
And the charge of the sons of Gershon in the tabernacle of the congregation shall be the tabernacle, and the tent, the covering thereof, and the hanging for the door of the tabernacle of the congregation,

(Numbers 3:26)
And the hangings of the court, and the curtain for the door of the court, which is by the tabernacle, and by the altar round about, and the cords of it for all the service thereof.

(Numbers 3:27)
And of Kohath was the family of the Amramites, and the family of the Izeharites, and the family of the Hebronites, and the family of the Uzzielites: these are the families of the Kohathites.

(Numbers 3:28)
In the number of all the males, from a month old and upward,

were eight thousand and six hundred, keeping the charge of the sanctuary.

(Numbers 3:29)
The families of the sons of Kohath shall pitch on the side of the tabernacle southward.

(Numbers 3:30)
And the chief of the house of the father of the families of the Kohathites shall be Elizaphan the son of Uzziel.

(Numbers 3:31)
And their charge shall be the ark, and the table, and the candlestick, and the altars, and the vessels of the sanctuary wherewith they minister, and the hanging, and all the service thereof.

(Numbers 3:32)
And Eleazar the son of Aaron the priest shall be chief over the chief of the Levites, and have the oversight of them that keep the charge of the sanctuary.

(Numbers 3:33)
Of Merari was the family of the Mahlites, and the family of the Mushites: these are the families of Merari.

(Numbers 3:34)
And those that were numbered of them, according to the number of all the males, from a month old and upward, were six thousand and two hundred.

(Numbers 3:35)
And the chief of the house of the father of the families of

Merari was Zuriel the son of Abihail: these shall pitch on the side of the tabernacle northward.

(Numbers 3:36)

And under the custody and charge of the sons of Merari shall be the boards of the tabernacle, and the bars thereof, and the pillars thereof, and the sockets thereof, and all the vessels thereof, and all that serves there,

(Numbers 3:37)

And the pillars of the court round about, and their sockets, and their pins, and their cords.

(Numbers 3:38)

But those that encamp before the tabernacle toward the east, even before the tabernacle of the congregation eastward, shall be Moses, and Aaron and his sons, keeping the charge of the sanctuary for the charge of the children of Israel; and the stranger that comes nigh shall be put to death.

(Numbers 3:39)

All that were numbered of the Levites, which Moses and Aaron numbered at the commandment of the LORD, throughout their families, all the males from a month old and upward, were twenty and two thousand.

(Numbers 3:40)

And the LORD said to Moses, Number all the firstborn of the males of the children of Israel from a month old and upward, and take the number of their names.

(Numbers 3:41)

And you shall take the Levites for me (I am the LORD) instead of all the firstborn among the children of Israel; and the cattle of the Levites instead of all the firstlings among the cattle of the children of Israel.

(Numbers 3:42)

And Moses numbered, as the LORD commanded him, all the firstborn among the children of Israel.

(Numbers 3:43)

And all the firstborn males by the number of names, from a month old and upward, of those that were numbered of them, were twenty and two thousand two hundred and threescore and thirteen.

(Numbers 3:44)

And the LORD spoke to Moses, saying,

(Numbers 3:45)

Take the Levites instead of all the firstborn among the children of Israel, and the cattle of the Levites instead of their cattle; and the Levites shall be mine: I am the LORD.

(Numbers 3:46)

And for those that are to be redeemed of the two hundred and threescore and thirteen of the firstborn of the children of Israel, which are more than the Levites;

(Numbers 3:47)

You shall even take five shekels apiece by the poll, after the shekel of the sanctuary shall you take them: (the shekel is twenty gerahs:)

(Numbers 3:48)

And you shall give the money, wherewith the odd number of them is to be redeemed, to Aaron and to his sons.

(Numbers 3:49)
And Moses took the redemption money of them that were over and above them that were redeemed by the Levites:

(Numbers 3:50)
Of the firstborn of the children of Israel took he the money; a thousand three hundred and threescore and five shekels, after the shekel of the sanctuary:

(Numbers 3:51)
And Moses gave the money of them that were redeemed to Aaron and to his sons, according to the word of the LORD, as the LORD commanded Moses.

Numbers: Chapter Four

(Numbers 4:1)
And the LORD spoke to Moses and to Aaron, saying,

(Numbers 4:2)
Take the sum of the sons of Kohath from among the sons of Levi, after their families, by the house of their fathers,

(Numbers 4:3)
From thirty years old and upward even until fifty years old, all that enter into the host, to do the work in the tabernacle of the congregation.

(Numbers 4:4)
This shall be the service of the sons of Kohath in the tabernacle of the congregation, about the most holy things:

(Numbers 4:5)
And when the camp sets forward, Aaron shall come, and his sons, and they shall take down the covering veil, and cover the ark of testimony with it:

(Numbers 4:6)
And shall put thereon the covering of badgers' skins, and shall spread over it a cloth wholly of blue, and shall put in the staves thereof.

(Numbers 4:7)
And upon the table of shewbread they shall spread a cloth of blue, and put thereon the dishes, and the spoons, and the

bowls, and covers to cover withal: and the continual bread shall be thereon:

(Numbers 4:8)

And they shall spread upon them a cloth of scarlet, and cover the same with a covering of badgers' skins, and shall put in the staves thereof.

(Numbers 4:9)

And they shall take a cloth of blue, and cover the candlestick of the light, and his lamps, and his tongs, and his snuffdishes, and all the oil vessels thereof, wherewith they minister to it:

(Numbers 4:10)

And they shall put it and all the vessels thereof within a covering of badgers' skins, and shall put it upon a bar.

(Numbers 4:11)

And upon the golden altar they shall spread a cloth of blue, and cover it with a covering of badgers' skins, and shall put to the staves thereof:

(Numbers 4:12)

And they shall take all the instruments of ministry, wherewith they minister in the sanctuary, and put them in a cloth of blue, and cover them with a covering of badgers' skins, and shall put them on a bar:

(Numbers 4:13)

And they shall take away the ashes from the altar, and spread a purple cloth thereon:

(Numbers 4:14)

And they shall put upon it all the vessels thereof, wherewith they minister about it, even the censers, the fleshhooks, and the shovels, and the basins, all the vessels of the altar; and they shall spread upon it a covering of badgers' skins, and put to the staves of it.

(Numbers 4:15)

And when Aaron and his sons have made an end of covering the sanctuary, and all the vessels of the sanctuary, as the camp is to set forward; after that, the sons of Kohath shall come to bear it: but they shall not touch any holy thing, lest they die. These things are the burden of the sons of Kohath in the tabernacle of the congregation.

(Numbers 4:16)

And to the office of Eleazar the son of Aaron the priest pertains the oil for the light, and the sweet incense, and the daily meat offering, and the anointing oil, and the oversight of all the tabernacle, and of all that therein is, in the sanctuary, and in the vessels thereof.

(Numbers 4:17)

And the LORD spoke to Moses and to Aaron, saying,

(Numbers 4:18)

Cut you not off the tribe of the families of the Kohathites from among the Levites:

(Numbers 4:19)

But thus do to them, that they may live, and not die, when they approach to the most holy things: Aaron and his sons shall go in, and appoint them every one to his service and to his burden:

(Numbers 4:20)
But they shall not go in to see when the holy things are covered, lest they die.

(Numbers 4:21)
And the LORD spoke to Moses, saying,

(Numbers 4:22)
Take also the sum of the sons of Gershon, throughout the houses of their fathers, by their families;

(Numbers 4:23)
From thirty years old and upward until fifty years old shall you number them; all that enter in to perform the service, to do the work in the tabernacle of the congregation.

(Numbers 4:24)
This is the service of the families of the Gershonites, to serve, and for burdens:

(Numbers 4:25)
And they shall bear the curtains of the tabernacle, and the tabernacle of the congregation, his covering, and the covering of the badgers' skins that is above upon it, and the hanging for the door of the tabernacle of the congregation,

(Numbers 4:26)
And the hangings of the court, and the hanging for the door of the gate of the court, which is by the tabernacle and by the altar round about, and their cords, and all the instruments of their service, and all that is made for them: so shall they serve.

(Numbers 4:27)
At the appointment of Aaron and his sons shall be all the

service of the sons of the Gershonites, in all their burdens, and in all their service: and you shall appoint to them in charge all their burdens.

(Numbers 4:28)
This is the service of the families of the sons of Gershon in the tabernacle of the congregation: and their charge shall be under the hand of Ithamar the son of Aaron the priest.

(Numbers 4:29)
As for the sons of Merari, you shall number them after their families, by the house of their fathers;

(Numbers 4:30)
From thirty years old and upward even to fifty years old shall you number them, every one that enters into the service, to do the work of the tabernacle of the congregation.

(Numbers 4:31)
And this is the charge of their burden, according to all their service in the tabernacle of the congregation; the boards of the tabernacle, and the bars thereof, and the pillars thereof, and sockets thereof,

(Numbers 4:32)
And the pillars of the court round about, and their sockets, and their pins, and their cords, with all their instruments, and with all their service: and by name you shall reckon the instruments of the charge of their burden.

(Numbers 4:33)
This is the service of the families of the sons of Merari, according to all their service, in the tabernacle of the congregation, under the hand of Ithamar the son of Aaron the priest.

(Numbers 4:34)

And Moses and Aaron and the chief of the congregation numbered the sons of the Kohathites after their families, and after the house of their fathers,

(Numbers 4:35)

From thirty years old and upward even to fifty years old, every one that enters into the service, for the work in the tabernacle of the congregation:

(Numbers 4:36)

And those that were numbered of them by their families were two thousand seven hundred and fifty.

(Numbers 4:37)

These were they that were numbered of the families of the Kohathites, all that might do service in the tabernacle of the congregation, which Moses and Aaron did number according to the commandment of the LORD by the hand of Moses.

(Numbers 4:38)

And those that were numbered of the sons of Gershon, throughout their families, and by the house of their fathers,

(Numbers 4:39)

From thirty years old and upward even to fifty years old, every one that enters into the service, for the work in the tabernacle of the congregation,

(Numbers 4:40)

Even those that were numbered of them, throughout their families, by the house of their fathers, were two thousand and six hundred and thirty.

(Numbers 4:41)

These are they that were numbered of the families of the sons of Gershon, of all that might do service in the tabernacle of the congregation, whom Moses and Aaron did number according to the commandment of the LORD.

(Numbers 4:42)

And those that were numbered of the families of the sons of Merari, throughout their families, by the house of their fathers,

(Numbers 4:43)

From thirty years old and upward even to fifty years old, every one that enters into the service, for the work in the tabernacle of the congregation,

(Numbers 4:44)

Even those that were numbered of them after their families, were three thousand and two hundred.

(Numbers 4:45)

These are those that were numbered of the families of the sons of Merari, whom Moses and Aaron numbered according to the word of the LORD by the hand of Moses.

(Numbers 4:46)

All those that were numbered of the Levites, whom Moses and Aaron and the chief of Israel numbered, after their families, and after the house of their fathers,

(Numbers 4:47)

From thirty years old and upward even to fifty years old, every one that came to do the service of the ministry, and the service of the burden in the tabernacle of the congregation,

(Numbers 4:48)

Even those that were numbered of them, were eight thousand and five hundred and fourscore.

(Numbers 4:49)

According to the commandment of the LORD they were numbered by the hand of Moses, every one according to his service, and according to his burden: thus were they numbered of him, as the LORD commanded Moses.

Numbers: Chapter Five

(Numbers 5:1)

And the LORD spoke to Moses, saying,

(Numbers 5:2)

Command the children of Israel, that they put out of the camp every leper, and every one that has an issue, and whosoever is defiled by the dead:

(Numbers 5:3)

Both male and female shall you put out, without the camp shall you put them; that they defile not their camps, in the midst whereof I dwell.

(Numbers 5:4)

And the children of Israel did so, and put them out without the camp: as the LORD spoke to Moses, so did the children of Israel.

(Numbers 5:5)

And the LORD spoke to Moses, saying,

(Numbers 5:6)

Speak to the children of Israel, When a man or woman shall commit any sin that men commit, to do a trespass against the LORD, and that person be guilty;

(Numbers 5:7)

Then they shall confess their sin which they have done: and he shall recompense his trespass with the principal thereof, and add to it the fifth part thereof, and give it to him against whom he has trespassed.

(Numbers 5:8)

But if the man have no kinsman to recompense the trespass to, let the trespass be recompensed to the LORD, even to the priest; beside the ram of the atonement, whereby an atonement shall be made for him.

(Numbers 5:9)

And every offering of all the holy things of the children of Israel, which they bring to the priest, shall be his.

(Numbers 5:10)

And every man's hallowed things shall be his: whatsoever any man gives to the priest, it shall be his.

(Numbers 5:11)

And the LORD spoke to Moses, saying,

(Numbers 5:12)

Speak to the children of Israel, and say to them, If any man's wife go aside, and commit a trespass against him,

(Numbers 5:13)

And a man lie with her carnally, and it be hid from the eyes of her husband, and be kept close, and she be defiled, and there be no witness against her, neither she be taken with the manner;

(Numbers 5:14)

And the spirit of jealousy come upon him, and he be jealous of his wife, and she be defiled: or if the spirit of jealousy come upon him, and he be jealous of his wife, and she be not defiled:

(Numbers 5:15)

Then shall the man bring his wife to the priest, and he shall bring her offering for her, the tenth part of an ephah of barley meal; he shall pour no oil upon it, nor put frankincense thereon; for it is an offering of jealousy, an offering of memorial, bringing iniquity to remembrance.

(Numbers 5:16)

And the priest shall bring her near, and set her before the LORD:

(Numbers 5:17)

And the priest shall take holy water in an earthen vessel; and of the dust that is in the floor of the tabernacle the priest shall take, and put it into the water:

(Numbers 5:18)

And the priest shall set the woman before the LORD, and uncover the woman's head, and put the offering of memorial in her hands, which is the jealousy offering: and the priest shall have in his hand the bitter water that causes the curse:

(Numbers 5:19)

And the priest shall charge her by an oath, and say to the woman, If no man have lain with you, and if you have not gone aside to uncleanness with another instead of your husband, be you free from this bitter water that causes the curse:

(Numbers 5:20)

But if you have gone aside to another instead of your husband, and if you be defiled, and some man have lain with you beside your husband:

(Numbers 5:21)

Then the priest shall charge the woman with an oath of cursing, and the priest shall say to the woman, The LORD make you a curse and an oath among your people, when the LORD do make your thigh to rot, and your belly to swell;

(Numbers 5:22)

And this water that causes the curse shall go into your bowels, to make your belly to swell, and your thigh to rot: And the woman shall say, Amen, amen.

(Numbers 5:23)

And the priest shall write these curses in a book, and he shall blot them out with the bitter water:

(Numbers 5:24)

And he shall cause the woman to drink the bitter water that causes the curse: and the water that causes the curse shall enter into her, and become bitter.

(Numbers 5:25)

Then the priest shall take the jealousy offering out of the woman's hand, and shall wave the offering before the LORD, and offer it upon the altar:

(Numbers 5:26)

And the priest shall take an handful of the offering, even the memorial thereof, and burn it upon the altar, and afterward shall cause the woman to drink the water.

(Numbers 5:27)

And when he has made her to drink the water, then it shall come to pass, that, if she be defiled, and have done trespass against her husband, that the water that causes the curse shall enter into her, and become bitter, and her belly shall swell, and her thigh shall rot: and the woman shall be a curse among her people.

(Numbers 5:28)

And if the woman be not defiled, but be clean; then she shall be free, and shall conceive seed.

(Numbers 5:29)

This is the law of jealousies, when a wife goes aside to another instead of her husband, and is defiled;

(Numbers 5:30)

Or when the spirit of jealousy comes upon him, and he be jealous over his wife, and shall set the woman before the LORD, and the priest shall execute upon her all this law.

(Numbers 5:31)

Then shall the man be guiltless from iniquity, and this woman shall bear her iniquity.

Numbers: Chapter Six

(Numbers 6:1)
And the LORD spoke to Moses, saying,

(Numbers 6:2)
Speak to the children of Israel, and say to them, When either man or woman shall separate themselves to vow a vow of a Nazarite, to separate themselves to the LORD:

(Numbers 6:3)
He shall separate himself from wine and strong drink, and shall drink no vinegar of wine, or vinegar of strong drink, neither shall he drink any liquor of grapes, nor eat moist grapes, or dried.

(Numbers 6:4)
All the days of his separation shall he eat nothing that is made of the vine tree, from the kernels even to the husk.

(Numbers 6:5)
All the days of the vow of his separation there shall no razor come upon his head: until the days be fulfilled, in the which he separates himself to the LORD, he shall be holy, and shall let the locks of the hair of his head grow.

(Numbers 6:6)
All the days that he separates himself to the LORD he shall come at no dead body.

(Numbers 6:7)

He shall not make himself unclean for his father, or for his mother, for his brother, or for his sister, when they die: because the consecration of his God is upon his head.

(Numbers 6:8)

All the days of his separation he is holy to the LORD.

(Numbers 6:9)

And if any man die very suddenly by him, and he has defiled the head of his consecration; then he shall shave his head in the day of his cleansing, on the seventh day shall he shave it.

(Numbers 6:10)

And on the eighth day he shall bring two turtles, or two young pigeons, to the priest, to the door of the tabernacle of the congregation:

(Numbers 6:11)

And the priest shall offer the one for a sin offering, and the other for a burnt offering, and make an atonement for him, for that he sinned by the dead, and shall hallow his head that same day.

(Numbers 6:12)

And he shall consecrate to the LORD the days of his separation, and shall bring a lamb of the first year for a trespass offering: but the days that were before shall be lost, because his separation was defiled.

(Numbers 6:13)

And this is the law of the Nazarite, when the days of his separation are fulfilled: he shall be brought to the door of the tabernacle of the congregation:

(Numbers 6:14)

And he shall offer his offering to the LORD, one he lamb of the first year without blemish for a burnt offering, and one ewe lamb of the first year without blemish for a sin offering, and one ram without blemish for peace offerings,

(Numbers 6:15)

And a basket of unleavened bread, cakes of fine flour mingled with oil, and wafers of unleavened bread anointed with oil, and their meat offering, and their drink offerings.

(Numbers 6:16)

And the priest shall bring them before the LORD, and shall offer his sin offering, and his burnt offering:

(Numbers 6:17)

And he shall offer the ram for a sacrifice of peace offerings to the LORD, with the basket of unleavened bread: the priest shall offer also his meat offering, and his drink offering.

(Numbers 6:18)

And the Nazarite shall shave the head of his separation at the door of the tabernacle of the congregation, and shall take the hair of the head of his separation, and put it in the fire which is under the sacrifice of the peace offerings.

(Numbers 6:19)

And the priest shall take the sodden shoulder of the ram, and one unleavened cake out of the basket, and one unleavened wafer, and shall put them upon the hands of the Nazarite, after the hair of his separation is shaved:

(Numbers 6:20)

And the priest shall wave them for a wave offering before the

LORD: this is holy for the priest, with the wave breast and heave shoulder: and after that the Nazarite may drink wine.

(Numbers 6:21)
This is the law of the Nazarite who has vowed, and of his offering to the LORD for his separation, beside that his hand shall get: according to the vow which he vowed, so he must do after the law of his separation.

(Numbers 6:22)
And the LORD spoke to Moses, saying,

(Numbers 6:23)
Speak to Aaron and to his sons, saying, On this wise you shall bless the children of Israel, saying to them,

(Numbers 6:24)
The LORD bless you, and keep you:

(Numbers 6:25)
The LORD make his face shine upon you, and be gracious to you:

(Numbers 6:26)
The LORD lift up his countenance upon you, and give you peace.

(Numbers 6:27)
And they shall put my name upon the children of Israel; and I will bless them.

Numbers: Chapter Seven

(Numbers 7:1)

And it came to pass on the day that Moses had fully set up the tabernacle, and had anointed it, and sanctified it, and all the instruments thereof, both the altar and all the vessels thereof, and had anointed them, and sanctified them;

(Numbers 7:2)

That the princes of Israel, heads of the house of their fathers, who were the princes of the tribes, and were over them that were numbered, offered:

(Numbers 7:3)

And they brought their offering before the LORD, six covered wagons, and twelve oxen; a wagon for two of the princes, and for each one an ox: and they brought them before the tabernacle.

(Numbers 7:4)

And the LORD spoke to Moses, saying,

(Numbers 7:5)

Take it of them, that they may be to do the service of the tabernacle of the congregation; and you shall give them to the Levites, to every man according to his service.

(Numbers 7:6)

And Moses took the wagons and the oxen, and gave them to the Levites.

(Numbers 7:7)

Two wagons and four oxen he gave to the sons of Gershon, according to their service:

(Numbers 7:8)

And four wagons and eight oxen he gave to the sons of Merari, according to their service, under the hand of Ithamar the son of Aaron the priest.

(Numbers 7:9)

But to the sons of Kohath he gave none: because the service of the sanctuary belonging to them was that they should bear upon their shoulders.

(Numbers 7:10)

And the princes offered for dedicating of the altar in the day that it was anointed, even the princes offered their offering before the altar.

(Numbers 7:11)

And the LORD said to Moses, They shall offer their offering, each prince on his day, for the dedicating of the altar.

(Numbers 7:12)

And he that offered his offering the first day was Nahshon the son of Amminadab, of the tribe of Judah:

(Numbers 7:13)

And his offering was one silver charger, the weight thereof was an hundred and thirty shekels, one silver bowl of seventy shekels, after the shekel of the sanctuary; both of them were full of fine flour mingled with oil for a meat offering:

(Numbers 7:14)
One spoon of ten shekels of gold, full of incense:

(Numbers 7:15)
One young bullock, one ram, one lamb of the first year, for a burnt offering:

(Numbers 7:16)
One kid of the goats for a sin offering:

(Numbers 7:17)
And for a sacrifice of peace offerings, two oxen, five rams, five he goats, five lambs of the first year: this was the offering of Nahshon the son of Amminadab.

(Numbers 7:18)
On the second day Nethaneel the son of Zuar, prince of Issachar, did offer:

(Numbers 7:19)
He offered for his offering one silver charger, the weight whereof was an hundred and thirty shekels, one silver bowl of seventy shekels, after the shekel of the sanctuary; both of them full of fine flour mingled with oil for a meat offering:

(Numbers 7:20)
One spoon of gold of ten shekels, full of incense:

(Numbers 7:21)
One young bullock, one ram, one lamb of the first year, for a burnt offering:

(Numbers 7:22)
One kid of the goats for a sin offering:

(Numbers 7:23)
And for a sacrifice of peace offerings, two oxen, five rams, five he goats, five lambs of the first year: this was the offering of Nethaneel the son of Zuar.

(Numbers 7:24)
On the third day Eliab the son of Helon, prince of the children of Zebulun, did offer:

(Numbers 7:25)
His offering was one silver charger, the weight whereof was an hundred and thirty shekels, one silver bowl of seventy shekels, after the shekel of the sanctuary; both of them full of fine flour mingled with oil for a meat offering:

(Numbers 7:26)
One golden spoon of ten shekels, full of incense:

(Numbers 7:27)
One young bullock, one ram, one lamb of the first year, for a burnt offering:

(Numbers 7:28)
One kid of the goats for a sin offering:

(Numbers 7:29)
And for a sacrifice of peace offerings, two oxen, five rams, five he goats, five lambs of the first year: this was the offering of Eliab the son of Helon.

(Numbers 7:30)

On the fourth day Elizur the son of Shedeur, prince of the children of Reuben, did offer:

(Numbers 7:31)

His offering was one silver charger of the weight of an hundred and thirty shekels, one silver bowl of seventy shekels, after the shekel of the sanctuary; both of them full of fine flour mingled with oil for a meat offering:

(Numbers 7:32)

One golden spoon of ten shekels, full of incense:

(Numbers 7:33)

One young bullock, one ram, one lamb of the first year, for a burnt offering:

(Numbers 7:34)

One kid of the goats for a sin offering:

(Numbers 7:35)

And for a sacrifice of peace offerings, two oxen, five rams, five he goats, five lambs of the first year: this was the offering of Elizur the son of Shedeur.

(Numbers 7:36)

On the fifth day Shelumiel the son of Zurishaddai, prince of the children of Simeon, did offer:

(Numbers 7:37)

His offering was one silver charger, the weight whereof was an hundred and thirty shekels, one silver bowl of seventy shekels, after the shekel of the sanctuary; both of them full of fine flour mingled with oil for a meat offering:

(Numbers 7:38)
One golden spoon of ten shekels, full of incense:

(Numbers 7:39)
One young bullock, one ram, one lamb of the first year, for a burnt offering:

(Numbers 7:40)
One kid of the goats for a sin offering:

(Numbers 7:41)
And for a sacrifice of peace offerings, two oxen, five rams, five he goats, five lambs of the first year: this was the offering of Shelumiel the son of Zurishaddai.

(Numbers 7:42)
On the sixth day Eliasaph the son of Deuel, prince of the children of Gad, offered:

(Numbers 7:43)
His offering was one silver charger of the weight of an hundred and thirty shekels, a silver bowl of seventy shekels, after the shekel of the sanctuary; both of them full of fine flour mingled with oil for a meat offering:

(Numbers 7:44)
One golden spoon of ten shekels, full of incense:

(Numbers 7:45)
One young bullock, one ram, one lamb of the first year, for a burnt offering:

(Numbers 7:46)
One kid of the goats for a sin offering:

(Numbers 7:47)
And for a sacrifice of peace offerings, two oxen, five rams, five he goats, five lambs of the first year: this was the offering of Eliasaph the son of Deuel.

(Numbers 7:48)
On the seventh day Elishama the son of Ammihud, prince of the children of Ephraim, offered:

(Numbers 7:49)
His offering was one silver charger, the weight whereof was an hundred and thirty shekels, one silver bowl of seventy shekels, after the shekel of the sanctuary; both of them full of fine flour mingled with oil for a meat offering:

(Numbers 7:50)
One golden spoon of ten shekels, full of incense:

(Numbers 7:51)
One young bullock, one ram, one lamb of the first year, for a burnt offering:

(Numbers 7:52)
One kid of the goats for a sin offering:

(Numbers 7:53)
And for a sacrifice of peace offerings, two oxen, five rams, five he goats, five lambs of the first year: this was the offering of Elishama the son of Ammihud.

(Numbers 7:54)

On the eighth day offered Gamaliel the son of Pedahzur, prince of the children of Manasseh:

(Numbers 7:55)

His offering was one silver charger of the weight of an hundred and thirty shekels, one silver bowl of seventy shekels, after the shekel of the sanctuary; both of them full of fine flour mingled with oil for a meat offering:

(Numbers 7:56)

One golden spoon of ten shekels, full of incense:

(Numbers 7:57)

One young bullock, one ram, one lamb of the first year, for a burnt offering:

(Numbers 7:58)

One kid of the goats for a sin offering:

(Numbers 7:59)

And for a sacrifice of peace offerings, two oxen, five rams, five he goats, five lambs of the first year: this was the offering of Gamaliel the son of Pedahzur.

(Numbers 7:60)

On the ninth day Abidan the son of Gideoni, prince of the children of Benjamin, offered:

(Numbers 7:61)

His offering was one silver charger, the weight whereof was an hundred and thirty shekels, one silver bowl of seventy shekels, after the shekel of the sanctuary; both of them full of fine flour mingled with oil for a meat offering:

(Numbers 7:62)
One golden spoon of ten shekels, full of incense:

(Numbers 7:63)
One young bullock, one ram, one lamb of the first year, for a burnt offering:

(Numbers 7:64)
One kid of the goats for a sin offering:

(Numbers 7:65)
And for a sacrifice of peace offerings, two oxen, five rams, five he goats, five lambs of the first year: this was the offering of Abidan the son of Gideoni.

(Numbers 7:66)
On the tenth day Ahiezer the son of Ammishaddai, prince of the children of Dan, offered:

(Numbers 7:67)
His offering was one silver charger, the weight whereof was an hundred and thirty shekels, one silver bowl of seventy shekels, after the shekel of the sanctuary; both of them full of fine flour mingled with oil for a meat offering:

(Numbers 7:68)
One golden spoon of ten shekels, full of incense:

(Numbers 7:69)
One young bullock, one ram, one lamb of the first year, for a burnt offering:

(Numbers 7:70)
One kid of the goats for a sin offering:

(Numbers 7:71)
And for a sacrifice of peace offerings, two oxen, five rams, five he goats, five lambs of the first year: this was the offering of Ahiezer the son of Ammishaddai.

(Numbers 7:72)
On the eleventh day Pagiel the son of Ocran, prince of the children of Asher, offered:

(Numbers 7:73)
His offering was one silver charger, the weight whereof was an hundred and thirty shekels, one silver bowl of seventy shekels, after the shekel of the sanctuary; both of them full of fine flour mingled with oil for a meat offering:

(Numbers 7:74)
One golden spoon of ten shekels, full of incense:

(Numbers 7:75)
One young bullock, one ram, one lamb of the first year, for a burnt offering:

(Numbers 7:76)
One kid of the goats for a sin offering:

(Numbers 7:77)
And for a sacrifice of peace offerings, two oxen, five rams, five he goats, five lambs of the first year: this was the offering of Pagiel the son of Ocran.

(Numbers 7:78)
On the twelfth day Ahira the son of Enan, prince of the children of Naphtali, offered:

(Numbers 7:79)
His offering was one silver charger, the weight whereof was an hundred and thirty shekels, one silver bowl of seventy shekels, after the shekel of the sanctuary; both of them full of fine flour mingled with oil for a meat offering:

(Numbers 7:80)
One golden spoon of ten shekels, full of incense:

(Numbers 7:81)
One young bullock, one ram, one lamb of the first year, for a burnt offering:

(Numbers 7:82)
One kid of the goats for a sin offering:

(Numbers 7:83)
And for a sacrifice of peace offerings, two oxen, five rams, five he goats, five lambs of the first year: this was the offering of Ahira the son of Enan.

(Numbers 7:84)
This was the dedication of the altar, in the day when it was anointed, by the princes of Israel: twelve chargers of silver, twelve silver bowls, twelve spoons of gold:

(Numbers 7:85)
Each charger of silver weighing an hundred and thirty shekels, each bowl seventy: all the silver vessels weighed two thousand and four hundred shekels, after the shekel of the sanctuary:

(Numbers 7:86)

The golden spoons were twelve, full of incense, weighing ten shekels apiece, after the shekel of the sanctuary: all the gold of the spoons was an hundred and twenty shekels.

(Numbers 7:87)

All the oxen for the burnt offering were twelve bullocks, the rams twelve, the lambs of the first year twelve, with their meat offering: and the kids of the goats for sin offering twelve.

(Numbers 7:88)

And all the oxen for the sacrifice of the peace offerings were twenty and four bullocks, the rams sixty, the he goats sixty, the lambs of the first year sixty. This was the dedication of the altar, after that it was anointed.

(Numbers 7:89)

And when Moses was gone into the tabernacle of the congregation to speak with him, then he heard the voice of one speaking to him from off the mercy seat that was upon the ark of testimony, from between the two cherubims: and he spoke to him.

Numbers: Chapter Eight

(Numbers 8:1)
And the LORD spoke to Moses, saying,

(Numbers 8:2)
Speak to Aaron, and say to him, When you light the lamps, the seven lamps shall give light over against the candlestick.

(Numbers 8:3)
And Aaron did so; he lighted the lamps thereof over against the candlestick, as the LORD commanded Moses.

(Numbers 8:4)
And this work of the candlestick was of beaten gold, to the shaft thereof, to the flowers thereof, was beaten work: according to the pattern which the LORD had shewed Moses, so he made the candlestick.

(Numbers 8:5)
And the LORD spoke to Moses, saying,

(Numbers 8:6)
Take the Levites from among the children of Israel, and cleanse them.

(Numbers 8:7)
And thus shall you do to them, to cleanse them: Sprinkle water of purifying upon them, and let them shave all their flesh, and let them wash their clothes, and so make themselves clean.

(Numbers 8:8)

Then let them take a young bullock with his meat offering, even fine flour mingled with oil, and another young bullock shall you take for a sin offering.

(Numbers 8:9)

And you shall bring the Levites before the tabernacle of the congregation: and you shall gather the whole assembly of the children of Israel together:

(Numbers 8:10)

And you shall bring the Levites before the LORD: and the children of Israel shall put their hands upon the Levites:

(Numbers 8:11)

And Aaron shall offer the Levites before the LORD for an offering of the children of Israel, that they may execute the service of the LORD.

(Numbers 8:12)

And the Levites shall lay their hands upon the heads of the bullocks: and you shall offer the one for a sin offering, and the other for a burnt offering, to the LORD, to make an atonement for the Levites.

(Numbers 8:13)

And you shall set the Levites before Aaron, and before his sons, and offer them for an offering to the LORD.

(Numbers 8:14)

Thus shall you separate the Levites from among the children of Israel: and the Levites shall be mine.

(Numbers 8:15)

And after that shall the Levites go in to do the service of the tabernacle of the congregation: and you shall cleanse them, and offer them for an offering.

(Numbers 8:16)

For they are wholly given to me from among the children of Israel; instead of such as open every womb, even instead of the firstborn of all the children of Israel, have I taken them to me.

(Numbers 8:17)

For all the firstborn of the children of Israel are mine, both man and beast: on the day that I smote every firstborn in the land of Egypt I sanctified them for myself.

(Numbers 8:18)

And I have taken the Levites for all the firstborn of the children of Israel.

(Numbers 8:19)

And I have given the Levites as a gift to Aaron and to his sons from among the children of Israel, to do the service of the children of Israel in the tabernacle of the congregation, and to make an atonement for the children of Israel: that there be no plague among the children of Israel, when the children of Israel come nigh to the sanctuary.

(Numbers 8:20)

And Moses, and Aaron, and all the congregation of the children of Israel, did to the Levites according to all that the LORD commanded Moses concerning the Levites, so did the children of Israel to them.

(Numbers 8:21)

And the Levites were purified, and they washed their clothes; and Aaron offered them as an offering before the LORD; and Aaron made an atonement for them to cleanse them.

(Numbers 8:22)

And after that went the Levites in to do their service in the tabernacle of the congregation before Aaron, and before his sons: as the LORD had commanded Moses concerning the Levites, so did they to them.

(Numbers 8:23)

And the LORD spoke to Moses, saying,

(Numbers 8:24)

This is it that belongs to the Levites: from twenty and five years old and upward they shall go in to wait upon the service of the tabernacle of the congregation:

(Numbers 8:25)

And from the age of fifty years they shall cease waiting upon the service thereof, and shall serve no more:

(Numbers 8:26)

But shall minister with their brethren in the tabernacle of the congregation, to keep the charge, and shall do no service. Thus shall you do to the Levites touching their charge.

Numbers: Chapter Nine

(Numbers 9:1)
And the LORD spoke to Moses in the wilderness of Sinai, in the first month of the second year after they were come out of the land of Egypt, saying,

(Numbers 9:2)
Let the children of Israel also keep the passover at his appointed season.

(Numbers 9:3)
In the fourteenth day of this month, at even, you shall keep it in his appointed season: according to all the rites of it, and according to all the ceremonies thereof, shall you keep it.

(Numbers 9:4)
And Moses spoke to the children of Israel, that they should keep the passover.

(Numbers 9:5)
And they kept the passover on the fourteenth day of the first month at even in the wilderness of Sinai: according to all that the LORD commanded Moses, so did the children of Israel.

(Numbers 9:6)
And there were certain men, who were defiled by the dead body of a man, that they could not keep the passover on that day: and they came before Moses and before Aaron on that day:

(Numbers 9:7)
And those men said to him, We are defiled by the dead body of a man: why are we kept back, that we may not offer an offering of the LORD in his appointed season among the children of Israel?

(Numbers 9:8)
And Moses said to them, Stand still, and I will hear what the LORD will command concerning you.

(Numbers 9:9)
And the LORD spoke to Moses, saying,

(Numbers 9:10)
Speak to the children of Israel, saying, If any man of you or of your posterity shall be unclean by reason of a dead body, or be in a journey afar off, yet he shall keep the passover to the LORD.

(Numbers 9:11)
The fourteenth day of the second month at even they shall keep it, and eat it with unleavened bread and bitter herbs.

(Numbers 9:12)
They shall leave none of it to the morning, nor break any bone of it: according to all the ordinances of the passover they shall keep it.

(Numbers 9:13)
But the man that is clean, and is not in a journey, and forbears to keep the passover, even the same soul shall be cut off from among his people: because he brought not the offering of the LORD in his appointed season, that man shall bear his sin.

(Numbers 9:14)

And if a stranger shall sojourn among you, and will keep the passover to the LORD; according to the ordinance of the passover, and according to the manner thereof, so shall he do: you shall have one ordinance, both for the stranger, and for him that was born in the land.

(Numbers 9:15)

And on the day that the tabernacle was reared up the cloud covered the tabernacle, namely, the tent of the testimony: and at even there was upon the tabernacle as it were the appearance of fire, until the morning.

(Numbers 9:16)

So it was alway: the cloud covered it by day, and the appearance of fire by night.

(Numbers 9:17)

And when the cloud was taken up from the tabernacle, then after that the children of Israel journeyed: and in the place where the cloud abode, there the children of Israel pitched their tents.

(Numbers 9:18)

At the commandment of the LORD the children of Israel journeyed, and at the commandment of the LORD they pitched: as long as the cloud abode upon the tabernacle they rested in their tents.

(Numbers 9:19)

And when the cloud tarried long upon the tabernacle many days, then the children of Israel kept the charge of the LORD, and journeyed not.

(Numbers 9:20)

And so it was, when the cloud was a few days upon the tabernacle; according to the commandment of the LORD they abode in their tents, and according to the commandment of the LORD they journeyed.

(Numbers 9:21)

And so it was, when the cloud abode from even to the morning, and that the cloud was taken up in the morning, then they journeyed: whether it was by day or by night that the cloud was taken up, they journeyed.

(Numbers 9:22)

Or whether it were two days, or a month, or a year, that the cloud tarried upon the tabernacle, remaining thereon, the children of Israel abode in their tents, and journeyed not: but when it was taken up, they journeyed.

(Numbers 9:23)

At the commandment of the LORD they rested in the tents, and at the commandment of the LORD they journeyed: they kept the charge of the LORD, at the commandment of the LORD by the hand of Moses.

Numbers: Chapter Ten

(Numbers 10:1)
And the LORD spoke to Moses, saying,

(Numbers 10:2)
Make you two trumpets of silver; of a whole piece shall you make them: that you may use them for the calling of the assembly, and for the journeying of the camps.

(Numbers 10:3)
And when they shall blow with them, all the assembly shall assemble themselves to you at the door of the tabernacle of the congregation.

(Numbers 10:4)
And if they blow but with one trumpet, then the princes, which are heads of the thousands of Israel, shall gather themselves to you.

(Numbers 10:5)
When you blow an alarm, then the camps that lie on the east parts shall go forward.

(Numbers 10:6)
When you blow an alarm the second time, then the camps that lie on the south side shall take their journey: they shall blow an alarm for their journeys.

(Numbers 10:7)
But when the congregation is to be gathered together, you

shall blow, but you shall not sound an alarm.

(Numbers 10:8)

And the sons of Aaron, the priests, shall blow with the trumpets; and they shall be to you for an ordinance forever throughout your generations.

(Numbers 10:9)

And if you go to war in your land against the enemy that oppresses you, then you shall blow an alarm with the trumpets; and you shall be remembered before the LORD your God, and you shall be saved from your enemies.

(Numbers 10:10)

Also in the day of your gladness, and in your solemn days, and in the beginnings of your months, you shall blow with the trumpets over your burnt offerings, and over the sacrifices of your peace offerings; that they may be to you for a memorial before your God: I am the LORD your God.

(Numbers 10:11) (Jasher 83:25)

And it came to pass on the twentieth day of the second month, in the second year, that the cloud was taken up from off the tabernacle of the testimony.

(Numbers 10:12)

And the children of Israel took their journeys out of the wilderness of Sinai; and the cloud rested in the wilderness of Paran.

(Numbers 10:13)

And they first took their journey according to the commandment of the LORD by the hand of Moses.

(Numbers 10:14)

In the first place went the standard of the camp of the children of Judah according to their armies: and over his host was Nahshon the son of Amminadab.

(Numbers 10:15)

And over the host of the tribe of the children of Issachar was Nethaneel the son of Zuar.

(Numbers 10:16)

And over the host of the tribe of the children of Zebulun was Eliab the son of Helon.

(Numbers 10:17)

And the tabernacle was taken down; and the sons of Gershon and the sons of Merari set forward, bearing the tabernacle.

(Numbers 10:18)

And the standard of the camp of Reuben set forward according to their armies: and over his host was Elizur the son of Shedeur.

(Numbers 10:19)

And over the host of the tribe of the children of Simeon was Shelumiel the son of Zurishaddai.

(Numbers 10:20)

And over the host of the tribe of the children of Gad was Eliasaph the son of Deuel.

(Numbers 10:21)

And the Kohathites set forward, bearing the sanctuary: and the other did set up the tabernacle against they came.

(Numbers 10:22)

And the standard of the camp of the children of Ephraim set forward according to their armies: and over his host was Elishama the son of Ammihud.

(Numbers 10:23)

And over the host of the tribe of the children of Manasseh was Gamaliel the son of Pedahzur.

(Numbers 10:24)

And over the host of the tribe of the children of Benjamin was Abidan the son of Gideoni.

(Numbers 10:25)

And the standard of the camp of the children of Dan set forward, which was the rearward of all the camps throughout their hosts: and over his host was Ahiezer the son of Ammishaddai.

(Numbers 10:26)

And over the host of the tribe of the children of Asher was Pagiel the son of Ocran.

(Numbers 10:27)

And over the host of the tribe of the children of Naphtali was Ahira the son of Enan.

(Numbers 10:28)

Thus were the journeyings of the children of Israel according to their armies, when they set forward.

(Numbers 10:29)

And Moses said to Hobab, the son of Raguel the Midianite, Moses' father in law, We are journeying to the place of which the LORD said, I will give it you: come you with us, and we will do you good: for the LORD has spoken good concerning Israel.

(Numbers 10:30)

And he said to him, I will not go; but I will depart to mine own land, and to my kindred.

(Numbers 10:31)

And he said, Leave us not, I pray you; forasmuch as you know how we are to encamp in the wilderness, and you may be to us instead of eyes.

(Numbers 10:32)

And it shall be, if you go with us, yea, it shall be, that what goodness the LORD shall do to us, the same will we do to you.

(Numbers 10:33) (Jasher 83:26…)

And at that time the children of Israel departed from the mount of the LORD, continued their journey from the wilderness of Sinai, and they took three days' journey: and the ark of the covenant of the LORD went before them in the three days' journey, to search out a resting place for them.

(Numbers 10:34)

And the cloud of the LORD was upon them by day, when they went out of the camp.

(Numbers 10:35)

And it came to pass, when the ark set forward, that Moses said, Rise up, LORD, and let your enemies be scattered; and let them that hate you flee before you.

(Numbers 10:36)

And when it rested, he said, Return, O LORD, to the many thousands of Israel.

Numbers: Chapter Eleven

(Numbers 11:1)
And when the people complained, it displeased the LORD: and the LORD heard it; and his anger was kindled; and the fire of the LORD burnt among them, and consumed them that were in the uttermost parts of the camp.

(Numbers 11:2)
And the people cried to Moses; and when Moses prayed to the LORD, the fire was quenched.

(Numbers 11:3)
And he called the name of the place Taberah: because the fire of the LORD burnt among them.

(...Jasher 83:26...)
And the cloud rested upon the wilderness of Paran;

(Numbers 11:4)
And the mixed multitude that was among them fell a lusting: and the children of Israel also wept again, and said, Who shall give us flesh to eat?

(Numbers 11:5)
We remember the fish, which we did eat in Egypt freely; the cucumbers, and the melons, and the leeks, and the onions, and the garlic:

(Numbers 11:6)
But now our soul is dried away: there is nothing at all, beside

this manna, before our eyes.

(Numbers 11:7)
And the manna was as coriander seed, and the color thereof as the color of bdellium.

(Numbers 11:8)
And the people went about, and gathered it, and ground it in mills, or beat it in a mortar, and baked it in pans, and made cakes of it: and the taste of it was as the taste of fresh oil.

(Numbers 11:9)
And when the dew fell upon the camp in the night, the manna fell upon it.

(Numbers 11:10) (...Jasher 83:26)
Then Moses heard the people weep throughout their families, every man in the door of his tent: and the anger of the LORD was kindled greatly against Israel for they had provoked the Lord in asking him for meat, that they might eat; Moses also was displeased.

(Numbers 11:11)
And Moses said to the LORD, Why have you afflicted your servant? And why have I not found favor in your sight, that you lay the burden of all this people upon me?

(Numbers 11:12)
Have I conceived all this people? Have I begotten them, that you should say to me, Carry them in your bosom, as a nursing father bears the sucking child, to the land which you swore to their fathers?

(Numbers 11:13)

Where should I have flesh to give to all this people? For they weep to me, saying, Give us flesh, that we may eat.

(Numbers 11:14)

I am not able to bear all this people alone, because it is too heavy for me.

(Numbers 11:15)

And if you deal thus with me, kill me, I pray you, out of hand, if I have found favor in your sight; and let me not see my wretchedness.

(Numbers 11:16)

And the LORD said to Moses, Gather to me seventy men of the elders of Israel, whom you know to be the elders of the people, and officers over them; and bring them to the tabernacle of the congregation, that they may stand there with you.

(Numbers 11:17)

And I will come down and talk with you there: and I will take of the spirit which is upon you, and will put it upon them; and they shall bear the burden of the people with you, that you bear it not thyself alone.

(Numbers 11:18)

And say you to the people, Sanctify yourselves against tomorrow, and you shall eat flesh: for you have wept in the ears of the LORD, saying, Who shall give us flesh to eat? For it was well with us in Egypt: therefore the LORD will give you flesh, and you shall eat.

(Numbers 11:19)
You shall not eat one day, nor two days, nor five days, neither ten days, nor twenty days;

(Numbers 11:20)
But even a whole month, until it come out at your nostrils, and it be loathsome to you: because that you have despised the LORD which is among you, and have wept before him, saying, Why came we forth out of Egypt?

(Numbers 11:21)
And Moses said, The people, among whom I am, are six hundred thousand footmen; and you have said, I will give them flesh, that they may eat a whole month.

(Numbers 11:22)
Shall the flocks and the herds be slain for them, to suffice them? Or shall all the fish of the sea be gathered together for them, to suffice them?

(Numbers 11:23)
And the LORD said to Moses, Is the LORD'S hand waxed short? You shall see now whether my word shall come to pass to you or not.

(Numbers 11:24)
And Moses went out, and told the people the words of the LORD, and gathered the seventy men of the elders of the people, and set them round about the tabernacle.

(Numbers 11:25)
And the LORD came down in a cloud, and spoke to him, and took of the spirit that was upon him, and gave it to the seventy elders: and it came to pass, that, when the spirit rested upon

them, they prophesied, and did not cease.

(Numbers 11:26)
But there remained two of the men in the camp, the name of the one was Eldad, and the name of the other Medad: and the spirit rested upon them; and they were of them that were written, but went not out to the tabernacle: and they prophesied in the camp.

(Numbers 11:27)
And there ran a young man, and told Moses, and said, Eldad and Medad do prophesy in the camp.

(Numbers 11:28)
And Joshua the son of Nun, the servant of Moses, one of his young men, answered and said, My lord Moses, forbid them.

(Numbers 11:29)
And Moses said to him, Do you envy for my sake? Would God that all the LORD'S people were prophets, and that the LORD would put his spirit upon them!

(Numbers 11:30)
And Moses went into the camp, he and the elders of Israel.

(Numbers 11:31)
And there went forth a wind from the LORD, and brought quails from the sea, and let them fall by the camp, as it were a day's journey on this side, and as it were a day's journey on the other side, round about the camp, and as it were two cubits high upon the face of the earth.

(Numbers 11:32)
And the people stood up all that day, and all that night, and all

the next day, and they gathered the quails: he that gathered least gathered ten homers: and they spread them all abroad for themselves round about the camp.

(Jasher 83:27)
And the Lord hearkened to their voice, and gave them meat which they ate for one month.

(Numbers 11:33) (Jasher 83:28)
And after this, while the flesh was yet between their teeth, ere it was chewed, the wrath of the LORD was kindled against the people, and the LORD smote the people with a very great plague, and they were buried there in that place.

(Numbers 11:34) (Jasher 83:29)
And he and the children of Israel called the name of that place Kibrothhattaavah: because there they buried the people that lusted flesh.

(Numbers 11:35) (Jasher 83:30)
And the people journeyed from Kibrothhattaavah to Hazeroth, which is in the wilderness of Paran; and abode at Hazeroth.

Numbers: Chapter Twelve

(Numbers 12:1) (Jasher 83:31...)

And while the children of Israel were in Hazeroth, Miriam and Aaron spoke against Moses because of the Ethiopian woman whom he had married: for he had married an Ethiopian woman.

(Numbers 12:2)

And they said, Has the LORD indeed spoken only by Moses? Has he not spoken also by us? And the LORD heard it.

(Numbers 12:3)

(Now the man Moses was very meek, above all the men which were upon the face of the earth.)

(Numbers 12:4)

And the LORD spoke suddenly to Moses, and to Aaron, and to Miriam, Come out you three to the tabernacle of the congregation. And they three came out.

(Numbers 12:5)

And the LORD came down in the pillar of the cloud, and stood in the door of the tabernacle, and called Aaron and Miriam: and they both came forth.

(Numbers 12:6)

And he said, Hear now my words: If there be a prophet among you, I the LORD will make myself known to him in a vision, and will speak to him in a dream.

(Numbers 12:7)

My servant Moses is not so, who is faithful in all mine house.

(Numbers 12:8)

With him will I speak mouth to mouth, even apparently, and not in dark speeches; and the similitude of the LORD shall he behold: why then were you not afraid to speak against my servant Moses?

(Numbers 12:9) (...Jasher 83:31...)

And the anger of the LORD was kindled against them on account of Moses; and he departed.

(Numbers 12:10) (...Jasher 83:31)

And the cloud departed from off the tabernacle; and, behold, Miriam became leprous, white as snow: and Aaron looked upon Miriam, and, behold, she was leprous.

(Numbers 12:11)

And Aaron said to Moses, Alas, my lord, I beseech you, lay not the sin upon us, wherein we have done foolishly, and wherein we have sinned.

(Numbers 12:12)

Let her not be as one dead, of whom the flesh is half consumed when he comes out of his mother's womb.

(Numbers 12:13)

And Moses cried to the LORD, saying, Heal her now, O God, I beseech you.

(Numbers 12:14)

And the LORD said to Moses, If her father had but spit in

her face, should she not be ashamed seven days? Let her be shut out from the camp seven days, and after that let her be received in again.

(Numbers 12:15) (Jasher 83:32)
And Miriam was shut out from the camp seven days until she had been received again after her leprosy: and the people journeyed not till Miriam was brought in again.

(Numbers 12:16) (Jasher 83:33)
And afterward the people removed from Hazeroth, and pitched in the end of the wilderness of Paran.

Numbers: Chapter Thirteen

(Numbers 13:1) (Jasher 83:34...)

And at that time, the LORD spoke to Moses, saying,

(Numbers 13:2) (...Jasher 83:34)

Send twelve men from the children of Israel, that they may search the land of Canaan, which I give to the children of Israel: of every tribe of their fathers shall you send a man, every one a ruler among them.

(Numbers 13:3)

And Moses by the commandment of the LORD sent them from the wilderness of Paran: all those men were heads of the children of Israel.

(Numbers 13:4)

And these were their names: of the tribe of Reuben, Shammua the son of Zaccur.

(Numbers 13:5)

Of the tribe of Simeon, Shaphat the son of Hori.

(Numbers 13:6)

Of the tribe of Judah, Caleb the son of Jephunneh.

(Numbers 13:7)

Of the tribe of Issachar, Igal the son of Joseph.

(Numbers 13:8)

Of the tribe of Ephraim, Oshea the son of Nun.

(Numbers 13:9)
Of the tribe of Benjamin, Palti the son of Raphu.

(Numbers 13:10)
Of the tribe of Zebulun, Gaddiel the son of Sodi.

(Numbers 13:11)
Of the tribe of Joseph, namely, of the tribe of Manasseh, Gaddi the son of Susi.

(Numbers 13:12)
Of the tribe of Dan, Ammiel the son of Gemalli.

(Numbers 13:13)
Of the tribe of Asher, Sethur the son of Michael.

(Numbers 13:14)
Of the tribe of Naphtali, Nahbi the son of Vophsi.

(Numbers 13:15)
Of the tribe of Gad, Geuel the son of Machi.

(Numbers 13:16)
These are the names of the men which Moses sent to spy out the land. And Moses called Oshea the son of Nun Jehoshua.

(Numbers 13:17) (Jasher 83:35...)
And Moses sent them to spy out the land of Canaan, and said to them, Get you up this way southward, and go up into the mountain:

(Numbers 13:18)
And see the land, what it is; and the people that dwells therein,

whether they are strong or weak, few or many;

(Numbers 13:19)
And what the land is that they dwell in, whether it be good or bad; and what cities they are that they dwell in, whether in tents, or in strong holds;

(Numbers 13:20)
And what the land is, whether it be fat or lean, whether there be wood therein, or not. And be you of good courage, and bring of the fruit of the land. Now the time was the time of the first ripe grapes.

(Numbers 13:21) (...Jasher 83:35)
So they went up, and they came to the land of Canaan to search and examine it, and they examined the whole land from the wilderness of Zin to Rehob, as men come to Hamath.

(Numbers 13:22)
And they ascended by the south, and came to Hebron; where Ahiman, Sheshai, and Talmai, the children of Anak, were. (Now Hebron was built seven years before Zoan in Egypt.)

(Numbers 13:23)
And they came to the brook of Eshcol, and cut down from there a branch with one cluster of grapes, and they bare it between two upon a staff; and they brought of the pomegranates, and of the figs.

(Numbers 13:24)
The place was called the brook Eshcol, because of the cluster of grapes which the children of Israel cut down from there.

(Numbers 13:25) (Jasher 83:36...)

And they returned from searching of the land after forty days.

(Numbers 13:26) (...Jasher 83:36...)

And they went and came to Moses, and to Aaron, and to all the congregation of the children of Israel, to the wilderness of Paran, to Kadesh; and brought back word to them as it was in their hearts, and to all the congregation, and shewed them the fruit of the land.

(Numbers 13:27)

And they told him, and said, We came to the land whither you sent us, and surely it flows with milk and honey; and this is the fruit of it.

(Numbers 13:28)

Nevertheless the people be strong that dwell in the land, and the cities are walled, and very great: and moreover we saw the children of Anak there.

(Numbers 13:29)

The Amalekites dwell in the land of the south: and the Hittites, and the Jebusites, and the Amorites, dwell in the mountains: and the Canaanites dwell by the sea, and by the coast of Jordan.

(Numbers 13:30)

And Caleb stilled the people before Moses, and said, Let us go up at once, and possess it; for we are well able to overcome it.

(Numbers 13:31)

But the men that went up with him said, We be not able to go up against the people; for they are stronger than we.

(Numbers 13:32) (...Jasher 83:36...)

And ten of the men, they brought up an evil report of the land which they had searched to the children of Israel, saying, The land, through which we have gone to search it, is a land that eats up the inhabitants thereof; and all the people that we saw in it are men of a great stature.

(Numbers 13:33)

And there we saw the giants, the sons of Anak, which come of the giants: and we were in our own sight as grasshoppers, and so we were in their sight.

(...Jasher 83:36)

It is better for us to return to Egypt than to go to this land, a land that consumes its inhabitants.

Numbers: Chapter Fourteen

(Numbers 14:1)
And all the congregation lifted up their voice, and cried; and the people wept that night.

(Numbers 14:2)
And all the children of Israel murmured against Moses and against Aaron: and the whole congregation said to them, Would God that we had died in the land of Egypt! Or would God we had died in this wilderness!

(Numbers 14:3)
And why has the LORD brought us to this land, to fall by the sword, that our wives and our children should be a prey? Were it not better for us to return into Egypt?

(Numbers 14:4)
And they said one to another, Let us make a captain, and let us return into Egypt.

(Numbers 14:5)
Then Moses and Aaron fell on their faces before all the assembly of the congregation of the children of Israel.

(Numbers 14:6) (Jasher 83:37...)
And Joshua the son of Nun, and Caleb the son of Jephunneh, which were of them that searched the land, rent their clothes:

(Numbers 14:7) (...Jasher 83:37)
And they spoke to all the company of the children of Israel, saying, The land, which we passed through to search it, is an exceeding good land.

(Numbers 14:8) (Jasher 83:38)
If the LORD delight in us, then he will bring us into this land, and give it us; a land which flows with milk and honey.

(Numbers 14:9)
Only rebel not you against the LORD, neither fear you the people of the land; for they are bread for us: their defense is departed from them, and the LORD is with us: fear them not.

(Jasher 83:39)
But the children of Israel would not hearken to them, and they hearkened to the words of the ten men who had brought up an evil report of the land.

(Numbers 14:10)
And all the congregation bade stone them with stones. And the glory of the LORD appeared in the tabernacle of the congregation before all the children of Israel.

(Jasher 83:40...)
And the Lord heard the murmurings of the children of Israel and he was angry.

(Numbers 14:11)
And the LORD said to Moses, How long will this people provoke me? And how long will it be ere they believe me, for all the signs which I have shewed among them?

(Numbers 14:12)

I will smite them with the pestilence, and disinherit them, and will make of you a greater nation and mightier than they.

(Numbers 14:13)

And Moses said to the LORD, Then the Egyptians shall hear it, (for you brought up this people in your might from among them;)

(Numbers 14:14)

And they will tell it to the inhabitants of this land: for they have heard that you LORD are among this people, that you LORD are seen face to face, and that your cloud stands over them, and that you go before them, by day time in a pillar of a cloud, and in a pillar of fire by night.

(Numbers 14:15)

Now if you shall kill all this people as one man, then the nations which have heard the fame of you will speak, saying,

(Numbers 14:16)

Because the LORD was not able to bring this people into the land which he swore to them, therefore he has slain them in the wilderness.

(Numbers 14:17)

And now, I beseech you, let the power of my Lord be great, according as you have spoken, saying,

(Numbers 14:18)

The LORD is long-suffering, and of great mercy, forgiving iniquity and transgression, and by no means clearing the guilty, visiting the iniquity of the fathers upon the children to the third and fourth generation.

(Numbers 14:19)
Pardon, I beseech you, the iniquity of this people according to the greatness of your mercy, and as you have forgiven this people, from Egypt even until now.

(Numbers 14:20)
And the LORD said, I have pardoned according to your word:

(Numbers 14:21)
But as truly as I live, all the earth shall be filled with the glory of the LORD.

(...Jasher 83:40)
And the Lord swore, saying

(Jasher 83:41)
Surely not one man of this wicked generation shall see the land from twenty years old and upward excepting Caleb the son of Jephuneh and Joshua the son of Nun.

(Numbers 14:22)
Because all those men which have seen my glory, and my miracles, which I did in Egypt and in the wilderness, and have tempted me now these ten times, and have not hearkened to my voice;

(Numbers 14:23)
Surely they shall not see the land which I swore to their fathers, neither shall any of them that provoked me see it:

(Numbers 14:24)
But my servant Caleb, because he had another spirit with him, and has followed me fully, him will I bring into the land that he went into; and his seed shall possess it.

(Numbers 14:25)

(Now the Amalekites and the Canaanites dwelt in the valley.) Tomorrow turn you, and get you into the wilderness by the way of the Red sea.

(Numbers 14:26)

And the LORD spoke to Moses and to Aaron, saying,

(Numbers 14:27)

How long shall I bear with this evil congregation, which murmur against me? I have heard the murmurings of the children of Israel, which they murmur against me.

(Jasher 83:42...)
Surely this wicked generation shall perish in this wilderness, and their children shall come to the land and they shall possess it;

(Numbers 14:28)

Say to them, As truly as I live, says the LORD, as you have spoken in mine ears, so will I do to you:

(Numbers 14:29)

Your carcases shall fall in this wilderness; and all that were numbered of you, according to your whole number, from twenty years old and upward, which have murmured against me,

(Numbers 14:30)

Doubtless you shall not come into the land, concerning which I swore to make you dwell therein, save Caleb the son of Jephunneh, and Joshua the son of Nun.

(Numbers 14:31)
But your little ones, which you said should be a prey, them will I bring in, and they shall know the land which you have despised.

(Numbers 14:32)
But as for you, your carcases, they shall fall in this wilderness.

(Numbers 14:33)
And your children shall wander in the wilderness forty years, and bear your whoredoms, until your carcases be wasted in the wilderness.

(Numbers 14:34)
After the number of the days in which you searched the land, even forty days, each day for a year, shall you bear your iniquities, even forty years, and you shall know my breach of promise.

(Numbers 14:35)
I the LORD have said, I will surely do it to all this evil congregation, that are gathered together against me: in this wilderness they shall be consumed, and there they shall die.

(Numbers 14:36)
And the men, which Moses sent to search the land, who returned, and made all the congregation to murmur against him, by bringing up a slander upon the land,

(Numbers 14:37)
Even those men that did bring up the evil report upon the land, died by the plague before the LORD.

(Numbers 14:38)
But Joshua the son of Nun, and Caleb the son of Jephunneh, which were of the men that went to search the land, lived still.

(Numbers 14:39)
And Moses told these sayings to all the children of Israel: and the people mourned greatly.

(Numbers 14:40)
And they rose up early in the morning, and went up into the top of the mountain, saying, Lo, we be here, and will go up to the place which the LORD has promised: for we have sinned.

(Numbers 14:41)
And Moses said, Why now do you transgress the commandment of the LORD? But it shall not prosper.

(Numbers 14:42)
Go not up, for the LORD is not among you; that you be not smitten before your enemies.

(Numbers 14:43)
For the Amalekites and the Canaanites are there before you, and you shall fall by the sword: because you are turned away from the LORD, therefore the LORD will not be with you.

(Numbers 14:44)
But they presumed to go up to the hill top: nevertheless the ark of the covenant of the LORD, and Moses, departed not out of the camp.

(Numbers 14:45)
Then the Amalekites came down, and the Canaanites which

dwelt in that hill, and smote them, and discomfited them, even to Hormah.

(...Jasher 83:42)
So the anger of the Lord was kindled against Israel and he made them wander in the wilderness for forty years until the end of that wicked generation, because they did not follow the Lord.

(Jasher 83:43)
And the people dwelt in the wilderness of Paran a long time, and they afterward proceeded to the wilderness by the way of the Red Sea.

Numbers: Chapter Fifteen

(Numbers 15:1)
And the LORD spoke to Moses, saying,

(Numbers 15:2)
Speak to the children of Israel, and say to them, When you be come into the land of your habitations, which I give to you,

(Numbers 15:3)
And will make an offering by fire to the LORD, a burnt offering, or a sacrifice in performing a vow, or in a freewill offering, or in your solemn feasts, to make a sweet savor to the LORD, of the herd, or of the flock:

(Numbers 15:4)
Then shall he that offers his offering to the LORD bring a meat offering of a tenth deal of flour mingled with the fourth part of a hin of oil.

(Numbers 15:5)
And the fourth part of a hin of wine for a drink offering shall you prepare with the burnt offering or sacrifice, for one lamb.

(Numbers 15:6)
Or for a ram, you shall prepare for a meat offering two tenth deals of flour mingled with the third part of a hin of oil.

(Numbers 15:7)
And for a drink offering you shall offer the third part of a hin of wine, for a sweet savor to the LORD.

(Numbers 15:8)
And when you prepare a bullock for a burnt offering, or for a sacrifice in performing a vow, or peace offerings to the LORD:

(Numbers 15:9)
Then shall he bring with a bullock a meat offering of three tenth deals of flour mingled with half a hin of oil.

(Numbers 15:10)
And you shall bring for a drink offering half a hin of wine, for an offering made by fire, of a sweet savor to the LORD.

(Numbers 15:11)
Thus shall it be done for one bullock, or for one ram, or for a lamb, or a kid.

(Numbers 15:12)
According to the number that you shall prepare, so shall you do to every one according to their number.

(Numbers 15:13)
All that are born of the country shall do these things after this manner, in offering an offering made by fire, of a sweet savor to the LORD.

(Numbers 15:14)
And if a stranger sojourn with you, or whosoever be among you in your generations, and will offer an offering made by fire, of a sweet savor to the LORD; as you do, so he shall do.

(Numbers 15:15)
One ordinance shall be both for you of the congregation, and also for the stranger that sojourns with you, an ordinance

forever in your generations: as you are, so shall the stranger be before the LORD.

(Numbers 15:16)
One law and one manner shall be for you, and for the stranger that sojourns with you.

(Numbers 15:17)
And the LORD spoke to Moses, saying,

(Numbers 15:18)
Speak to the children of Israel, and say to them, When you come into the land whither I bring you,

(Numbers 15:19)
Then it shall be, that, when you eat of the bread of the land, you shall offer up an heave offering to the LORD.

(Numbers 15:20)
You shall offer up a cake of the first of your dough for an heave offering: as you do the heave offering of the threshing floor, so shall you heave it.

(Numbers 15:21)
Of the first of your dough you shall give to the LORD an heave offering in your generations.

(Numbers 15:22)
And if you have erred, and not observed all these commandments, which the LORD has spoken to Moses,

(Numbers 15:23)
Even all that the LORD has commanded you by the hand of

Moses, from the day that the LORD commanded Moses, and henceforward among your generations;

(Numbers 15:24)
Then it shall be, if ought be committed by ignorance without the knowledge of the congregation, that all the congregation shall offer one young bullock for a burnt offering, for a sweet savor to the LORD, with his meat offering, and his drink offering, according to the manner, and one kid of the goats for a sin offering.

(Numbers 15:25)
And the priest shall make an atonement for all the congregation of the children of Israel, and it shall be forgiven them; for it is ignorance: and they shall bring their offering, a sacrifice made by fire to the LORD, and their sin offering before the LORD, for their ignorance:

(Numbers 15:26)
And it shall be forgiven all the congregation of the children of Israel, and the stranger that sojourns among them; seeing all the people were in ignorance.

(Numbers 15:27)
And if any soul sin through ignorance, then he shall bring a she goat of the first year for a sin offering.

(Numbers 15:28)
And the priest shall make an atonement for the soul that sins ignorantly, when he sins by ignorance before the LORD, to make an atonement for him; and it shall be forgiven him.

(Numbers 15:29)
You shall have one law for him that sins through ignorance,

both for him that is born among the children of Israel, and for the stranger that sojourns among them.

(Numbers 15:30)

But the soul that does ought presumptuously, whether he be born in the land, or a stranger, the same reproaches the LORD; and that soul shall be cut off from among his people.

(Numbers 15:31)

Because he has despised the word of the LORD, and has broken his commandment, that soul shall utterly be cut off; his iniquity shall be upon him.

(Numbers 15:32)

And while the children of Israel were in the wilderness, they found a man that gathered sticks upon the sabbath day.

(Numbers 15:33)

And they that found him gathering sticks brought him to Moses and Aaron, and to all the congregation.

(Numbers 15:34)

And they put him in ward, because it was not declared what should be done to him.

(Numbers 15:35)

And the LORD said to Moses, The man shall be surely put to death: all the congregation shall stone him with stones without the camp.

(Numbers 15:36)

And all the congregation brought him without the camp, and stoned him with stones, and he died; as the LORD commanded Moses.

(Numbers 15:37)
And the LORD spoke to Moses, saying,

(Numbers 15:38)
Speak to the children of Israel, and bid them that they make them fringes in the borders of their garments throughout their generations, and that they put upon the fringe of the borders a ribbon of blue:

(Numbers 15:39)
And it shall be to you for a fringe, that you may look upon it, and remember all the commandments of the LORD, and do them; and that you seek not after your own heart and your own eyes, after which you use to go a whoring:

(Numbers 15:40)
That you may remember, and do all my commandments, and be holy to your God.

(Numbers 15:41)
I am the LORD your God, which brought you out of the land of Egypt, to be your God: I am the LORD your God.

Numbers: Chapter Sixteen

(Numbers 16:1) (Jasher 84:1...)

Now at that time Korah, the son of Izhar, the son of Kohath, the son of Levi, and Dathan and Abiram, the sons of Eliab, and On, the son of Peleth, sons of Reuben, took many men of the children of Israel:

(Numbers 16:2) (...Jasher 84:1...)

And they rose up before Moses, with certain of the children of Israel, two hundred and fifty princes of the assembly, famous in the congregation, men of renown:

(Numbers 16:3) (...Jasher 84:1)

And they gathered themselves together against Moses and against Aaron, and quarreled with Moses and Aaron and the whole congregation and said to them, You take too much upon you, seeing all the congregation are holy, every one of them, and the LORD is among them: why then lift you up yourselves above the congregation of the LORD?

(Numbers 16:4)

And when Moses heard it, he fell upon his face:

(Numbers 16:5)

And he spoke to Korah and to all his company, saying, Even tomorrow the LORD will shew who are his, and who is holy; and will cause him to come near to him: even him whom he has chosen will he cause to come near to him.

(Numbers 16:6)
This do; Take you censers, Korah, and all his company;

(Numbers 16:7)
And put fire therein, and put incense in them before the LORD tomorrow: and it shall be that the man whom the LORD do choose, he shall be holy: you take too much upon you, you sons of Levi.

(Numbers 16:8)
And Moses said to Korah, Hear, I pray you, you sons of Levi:

(Numbers 16:9)
Does it seem but a small thing to you, that the God of Israel has separated you from the congregation of Israel, to bring you near to himself to do the service of the tabernacle of the LORD, and to stand before the congregation to minister to them?

(Numbers 16:10)
And he has brought you near to him, and all your brethren the sons of Levi with you: and seek you the priesthood also?

(Numbers 16:11)
For which cause both you and all your company are gathered together against the LORD: and what is Aaron, that you murmur against him?

(Numbers 16:12)
And Moses sent to call Dathan and Abiram, the sons of Eliab: which said, We will not come up:

(Numbers 16:13)
Is it a small thing that you have brought us up out of a land

that flows with milk and honey, to kill us in the wilderness, except you make thyself altogether a prince over us?

(Numbers 16:14)

Moreover you have not brought us into a land that flows with milk and honey, or given us inheritance of fields and vineyards: wilt you put out the eyes of these men? We will not come up.

(Numbers 16:15)

And Moses was very wroth, and said to the LORD, Respect not you their offering: I have not taken one donkey from them, neither have I hurt one of them.

(Numbers 16:16)

And Moses said to Korah, Be you and all your company before the LORD, you, and they, and Aaron, tomorrow:

(Numbers 16:17)

And take every man his censer, and put incense in them, and bring you before the LORD every man his censer, two hundred and fifty censers; you also, and Aaron, each of you his censer.

(Numbers 16:18)

And they took every man his censer, and put fire in them, and laid incense thereon, and stood in the door of the tabernacle of the congregation with Moses and Aaron.

(Numbers 16:19)

And Korah gathered all the congregation against them to the door of the tabernacle of the congregation: and the glory of the LORD appeared to all the congregation.

(Numbers 16:20) (Jasher 84:2...)

And the LORD was angry with them and spoke to Moses and to Aaron, saying,

(Numbers 16:21)

Separate yourselves from among this congregation, that I may consume them in a moment.

(Numbers 16:22)

And they fell upon their faces, and said, O God, the God of the spirits of all flesh, shall one man sin, and wilt you be wroth with all the congregation?

(Numbers 16:23)

And the LORD spoke to Moses, saying,

(Numbers 16:24)

Speak to the congregation, saying, Get you up from about the tabernacle of Korah, Dathan, and Abiram.

(Numbers 16:25)

And Moses rose up and went to Dathan and Abiram; and the elders of Israel followed him.

(Numbers 16:26)

And he spoke to the congregation, saying, Depart, I pray you, from the tents of these wicked men, and touch nothing of theirs, lest you be consumed in all their sins.

(Numbers 16:27)

So they got up from the tabernacle of Korah, Dathan, and Abiram, on every side: and Dathan and Abiram came out, and stood in the door of their tents, and their wives, and their sons, and their little children.

(Numbers 16:28)

And Moses said, Hereby you shall know that the LORD has sent me to do all these works; for I have not done them of mine own mind.

(Numbers 16:29)

If these men die the common death of all men, or if they are visited after the visitation of all men; then the LORD has not sent me.

(Numbers 16:30)

But if the LORD make a new thing, and the earth open her mouth, and swallow them up, with all that appertain to them, and they go down quick into the pit; then you shall understand that these men have provoked the LORD.

(Numbers 16:31)

And it came to pass, as he had made an end of speaking all these words, that the ground clave asunder that was under them:

(Numbers 16:32) (...Jasher 84:2)

And the earth opened her mouth, and swallowed them up, and their houses, and all the men that appertained to Korah, and all their goods.

(Numbers 16:33)

They, and all that appertained to them, went down alive into the pit, and the earth closed upon them: and they perished from among the congregation.

(Numbers 16:34)

And all Israel that were round about them fled at the cry of them: for they said, Lest the earth swallow us up also.

(Numbers 16:35)

And there came out a fire from the LORD, and consumed the two hundred and fifty men that offered incense.

(Numbers 16:36)

And the LORD spoke to Moses, saying,

(Numbers 16:37)

Speak to Eleazar the son of Aaron the priest, that he take up the censers out of the burning, and scatter you the fire yonder; for they are hallowed.

(Numbers 16:38)

The censers of these sinners against their own souls, let them make them broad plates for a covering of the altar: for they offered them before the LORD, therefore they are hallowed: and they shall be a sign to the children of Israel.

(Numbers 16:39)

And Eleazar the priest took the brazen censers, wherewith they that were burnt had offered; and they were made broad plates for a covering of the altar:

(Numbers 16:40)

To be a memorial to the children of Israel, that no stranger, which is not of the seed of Aaron, come near to offer incense before the LORD; that he be not as Korah, and as his company: as the LORD said to him by the hand of Moses.

(Numbers 16:41)

But on the morrow all the congregation of the children of Israel murmured against Moses and against Aaron, saying, You have killed the people of the LORD.

(Numbers 16:42)

And it came to pass, when the congregation was gathered against Moses and against Aaron, that they looked toward the tabernacle of the congregation: and, behold, the cloud covered it, and the glory of the LORD appeared.

(Numbers 16:43)

And Moses and Aaron came before the tabernacle of the congregation.

(Numbers 16:44)

And the LORD spoke to Moses, saying,

(Numbers 16:45)

Get you up from among this congregation, that I may consume them as in a moment. And they fell upon their faces.

(Numbers 16:46)

And Moses said to Aaron, Take a censer, and put fire therein from off the altar, and put on incense, and go quickly to the congregation, and make an atonement for them: for there is wrath gone out from the LORD; the plague is begun.

(Numbers 16:47)

And Aaron took as Moses commanded, and ran into the midst of the congregation; and, behold, the plague was begun among the people: and he put on incense, and made an atonement for the people.

(Numbers 16:48)

And he stood between the dead and the living; and the plague was stayed.

(Numbers 16:49)

Now they that died in the plague were fourteen thousand and seven hundred, beside them that died about the matter of Korah.

(Numbers 16:50)

And Aaron returned to Moses to the door of the tabernacle of the congregation: and the plague was stayed.

(Jasher 84:3)

And after this God made the people go round by the way of Mount Seir for a long time.

Numbers: Chapter Seventeen

(Numbers 17:1)

And the LORD spoke to Moses, saying,

(Numbers 17:2)

Speak to the children of Israel, and take of every one of them a rod according to the house of their fathers, of all their princes according to the house of their fathers twelve rods: write you every man's name upon his rod.

(Numbers 17:3)

And you shall write Aaron's name upon the rod of Levi: for one rod shall be for the head of the house of their fathers.

(Numbers 17:4)

And you shall lay them up in the tabernacle of the congregation before the testimony, where I will meet with you.

(Numbers 17:5)

And it shall come to pass, that the man's rod, whom I shall choose, shall blossom: and I will make to cease from me the murmurings of the children of Israel, whereby they murmur against you.

(Numbers 17:6)

And Moses spoke to the children of Israel, and every one of their princes gave him a rod apiece, for each prince one, according to their fathers' houses, even twelve rods: and the rod of Aaron was among their rods.

(Numbers 17:7)

And Moses laid up the rods before the LORD in the tabernacle of witness.

(Numbers 17:8)

And it came to pass, that on the morrow Moses went into the tabernacle of witness; and, behold, the rod of Aaron for the house of Levi was budded, and brought forth buds, and bloomed blossoms, and yielded almonds.

(Numbers 17:9)

And Moses brought out all the rods from before the LORD to all the children of Israel: and they looked, and took every man his rod.

(Numbers 17:10)

And the LORD said to Moses, Bring Aaron's rod again before the testimony, to be kept for a token against the rebels; and you shall quite take away their murmurings from me, that they die not.

(Numbers 17:11)

And Moses did so: as the LORD commanded him, so did he.

(Numbers 17:12)

And the children of Israel spoke to Moses, saying, Behold, we die, we perish, we all perish.

(Numbers 17:13)

Whosoever comes any thing near to the tabernacle of the LORD shall die: shall we be consumed with dying?

Numbers: Chapter Eighteen

(Numbers 18:1)

And the LORD said to Aaron, You and your sons and your father's house with you shall bear the iniquity of the sanctuary: and you and your sons with you shall bear the iniquity of your priesthood.

(Numbers 18:2)

And your brethren also of the tribe of Levi, the tribe of your father, bring you with you, that they may be joined to you, and minister to you: but you and your sons with you shall minister before the tabernacle of witness.

(Numbers 18:3)

And they shall keep your charge, and the charge of all the tabernacle: only they shall not come nigh the vessels of the sanctuary and the altar, that neither they, nor you also, die.

(Numbers 18:4)

And they shall be joined to you, and keep the charge of the tabernacle of the congregation, for all the service of the tabernacle: and a stranger shall not come nigh to you.

(Numbers 18:5)

And you shall keep the charge of the sanctuary, and the charge of the altar: that there be no wrath any more upon the children of Israel.

(Numbers 18:6)

And I, behold, I have taken your brethren the Levites from

among the children of Israel: to you they are given as a gift for the LORD, to do the service of the tabernacle of the congregation.

(Numbers 18:7)

Therefore you and your sons with you shall keep your priest's office for every thing of the altar, and within the veil; and you shall serve: I have given your priest's office to you as a service of gift: and the stranger that comes nigh shall be put to death.

(Numbers 18:8)

And the LORD spoke to Aaron, Behold, I also have given you the charge of mine heave offerings of all the hallowed things of the children of Israel; to you have I given them by reason of the anointing, and to your sons, by an ordinance forever.

(Numbers 18:9)

This shall be yours of the most holy things, reserved from the fire: every oblation of theirs, every meat offering of theirs, and every sin offering of theirs, and every trespass offering of theirs, which they shall render to me, shall be most holy for you and for your sons.

(Numbers 18:10)

In the most holy place shall you eat it; every male shall eat it: it shall be holy to you.

(Numbers 18:11)

And this is yours; the heave offering of their gift, with all the wave offerings of the children of Israel: I have given them to you, and to your sons and to your daughters with you, by a statute forever: every one that is clean in your house shall eat of it.

(Numbers 18:12)

All the best of the oil, and all the best of the wine, and of the wheat, the firstfruits of them which they shall offer to the LORD, them have I given you.

(Numbers 18:13)

And whatsoever is first ripe in the land, which they shall bring to the LORD, shall be yours; every one that is clean in your house shall eat of it.

(Numbers 18:14)

Every thing devoted in Israel shall be yours.

(Numbers 18:15)

Every thing that opens the matrix in all flesh, which they bring to the LORD, whether it be of men or beasts, shall be yours: nevertheless the firstborn of man shall you surely redeem, and the firstling of unclean beasts shall you redeem.

(Numbers 18:16)

And those that are to be redeemed from a month old shall you redeem, according to your estimation, for the money of five shekels, after the shekel of the sanctuary, which is twenty gerahs.

(Numbers 18:17)

But the firstling of a cow, or the firstling of a sheep, or the firstling of a goat, you shall not redeem; they are holy: you shall sprinkle their blood upon the altar, and shall burn their fat for an offering made by fire, for a sweet savor to the LORD.

(Numbers 18:18)

And the flesh of them shall be yours, as the wave breast and as the right shoulder are yours.

(Numbers 18:19)

All the heave offerings of the holy things, which the children of Israel offer to the LORD, have I given you, and your sons and your daughters with you, by a statute forever: it is a covenant of salt forever before the LORD to you and to your seed with you.

(Numbers 18:20)

And the LORD spoke to Aaron, You shall have no inheritance in their land, neither shall you have any part among them: I am your part and your inheritance among the children of Israel.

(Numbers 18:21)

And, behold, I have given the children of Levi all the tenth in Israel for an inheritance, for their service which they serve, even the service of the tabernacle of the congregation.

(Numbers 18:22)

Neither must the children of Israel henceforth come nigh the tabernacle of the congregation, lest they bear sin, and die.

(Numbers 18:23)

But the Levites shall do the service of the tabernacle of the congregation, and they shall bear their iniquity: it shall be a statute forever throughout your generations, that among the children of Israel they have no inheritance.

(Numbers 18:24)

But the tithes of the children of Israel, which they offer as an heave offering to the LORD, I have given to the Levites to inherit: therefore I have said to them, Among the children of Israel they shall have no inheritance.

(Numbers 18:25)
And the LORD spoke to Moses, saying,

(Numbers 18:26)
Thus speak to the Levites, and say to them, When you take of the children of Israel the tithes which I have given you from them for your inheritance, then you shall offer up an heave offering of it for the LORD, even a tenth part of the tithe.

(Numbers 18:27)
And your heave offering shall be reckoned to you, as though it were the corn of the threshing floor, and as the fullness of the winepress.

(Numbers 18:28)
Thus you also shall offer an heave offering to the LORD of all your tithes, which you receive of the children of Israel; and you shall give thereof the LORD'S heave offering to Aaron the priest.

(Numbers 18:29)
Out of all your gifts you shall offer every heave offering of the LORD, of all the best thereof, even the hallowed part thereof out of it.

(Numbers 18:30)
Therefore you shall say to them, When you have heaved the best thereof from it, then it shall be counted to the Levites as the increase of the threshing floor, and as the increase of the winepress.

(Numbers 18:31)
And you shall eat it in every place, you and your households:

for it is your reward for your service in the tabernacle of the congregation.

(Numbers 18:32)

And you shall bear no sin by reason of it, when you have heaved from it the best of it: neither shall you pollute the holy things of the children of Israel, lest you die.

Numbers: Chapter Nineteen

(Numbers 19:1)
And the LORD spoke to Moses and to Aaron, saying,

(Numbers 19:2)
This is the ordinance of the law which the LORD has commanded, saying, Speak to the children of Israel, that they bring you a red heifer without spot, wherein is no blemish, and upon which never came yoke:

(Numbers 19:3)
And you shall give her to Eleazar the priest, that he may bring her forth without the camp, and one shall slay her before his face:

(Numbers 19:4)
And Eleazar the priest shall take of her blood with his finger, and sprinkle of her blood directly before the tabernacle of the congregation seven times:

(Numbers 19:5)
And one shall burn the heifer in his sight; her skin, and her flesh, and her blood, with her dung, shall he burn:

(Numbers 19:6)
And the priest shall take cedar wood, and hyssop, and scarlet, and cast it into the midst of the burning of the heifer.

(Numbers 19:7)
Then the priest shall wash his clothes, and he shall bathe his

flesh in water, and afterward he shall come into the camp, and the priest shall be unclean until the even.

(Numbers 19:8)
And he that burns her shall wash his clothes in water, and bathe his flesh in water, and shall be unclean until the even.

(Numbers 19:9)
And a man that is clean shall gather up the ashes of the heifer, and lay them up without the camp in a clean place, and it shall be kept for the congregation of the children of Israel for a water of separation: it is a purification for sin.

(Numbers 19:10)
And he that gathers the ashes of the heifer shall wash his clothes, and be unclean until the even: and it shall be to the children of Israel, and to the stranger that sojourns among them, for a statute forever.

(Numbers 19:11)
He that touches the dead body of any man shall be unclean seven days.

(Numbers 19:12)
He shall purify himself with it on the third day, and on the seventh day he shall be clean: but if he purify not himself the third day, then the seventh day he shall not be clean.

(Numbers 19:13)
Whosoever touches the dead body of any man that is dead, and purifies not himself, defiles the tabernacle of the LORD; and that soul shall be cut off from Israel: because the water of separation was not sprinkled upon him, he shall be unclean; his uncleanness is yet upon him.

(Numbers 19:14)
This is the law, when a man dies in a tent: all that come into the tent, and all that is in the tent, shall be unclean seven days.

(Numbers 19:15)
And every open vessel, which has no covering bound upon it, is unclean.

(Numbers 19:16)
And whosoever touches one that is slain with a sword in the open fields, or a dead body, or a bone of a man, or a grave, shall be unclean seven days.

(Numbers 19:17)
And for an unclean person they shall take of the ashes of the burnt heifer of purification for sin, and running water shall be put there in a vessel:

(Numbers 19:18)
And a clean person shall take hyssop, and dip it in the water, and sprinkle it upon the tent, and upon all the vessels, and upon the persons that were there, and upon him that touched a bone, or one slain, or one dead, or a grave:

(Numbers 19:19)
And the clean person shall sprinkle upon the unclean on the third day, and on the seventh day: and on the seventh day he shall purify himself, and wash his clothes, and bathe himself in water, and shall be clean at even.

(Numbers 19:20)
But the man that shall be unclean, and shall not purify himself, that soul shall be cut off from among the congregation, because he has defiled the sanctuary of the LORD: the water

of separation has not been sprinkled upon him; he is unclean.

(Numbers 19:21)

And it shall be a perpetual statute to them, that he that sprinkles the water of separation shall wash his clothes; and he that touches the water of separation shall be unclean until even.

(Numbers 19:22)

And whatsoever the unclean person touches shall be unclean; and the soul that touches it shall be unclean until even.

Numbers: Chapter Twenty

(Numbers 20:1)
Then came the children of Israel, even the whole congregation, into the desert of Zin in the first month: and the people abode in Kadesh; and Miriam died there, and was buried there.

(Numbers 20:2)
And there was no water for the congregation: and they gathered themselves together against Moses and against Aaron.

(Numbers 20:3)
And the people argued with Moses, and spoke, saying, Would God that we had died when our brethren died before the LORD!

(Numbers 20:4)
And why have you brought up the congregation of the LORD into this wilderness, that we and our cattle should die there?

(Numbers 20:5)
And why have you made us to come up out of Egypt, to bring us in to this evil place? It is no place of seed, or of figs, or of vines, or of pomegranates; neither is there any water to drink.

(Numbers 20:6)
And Moses and Aaron went from the presence of the assembly to the door of the tabernacle of the congregation, and they fell upon their faces: and the glory of the LORD appeared to them.

(Numbers 20:7)
And the LORD spoke to Moses, saying,

(Numbers 20:8)
Take the rod, and gather you the assembly together, you, and Aaron your brother, and speak you to the rock before their eyes; and it shall give forth his water, and you shall bring forth to them water out of the rock: so you shall give the congregation and their beasts drink.

(Numbers 20:9)
And Moses took the rod from before the LORD, as he commanded him.

(Numbers 20:10)
And Moses and Aaron gathered the congregation together before the rock, and he said to them, Hear now, you rebels; must we fetch you water out of this rock?

(Numbers 20:11)
And Moses lifted up his hand, and with his rod he smote the rock twice: and the water came out abundantly, and the congregation drank, and their beasts also.

(Numbers 20:12)
And the LORD spoke to Moses and Aaron, Because you believed me not, to sanctify me in the eyes of the children of Israel, therefore you shall not bring this congregation into the land which I have given them.

(Numbers 20:13)
This is the water of Meribah; because the children of Israel strove with the LORD, and he was sanctified in them.

(Jasher 84:4)
At that time the Lord said to Moses, Provoke not a war against the children of Esau, for I will not give to you of any thing belonging to them, as much as the sole of the foot could tread upon, for I have given Mount Seir for an inheritance to Esau.

(Jasher 84:5)
Therefore did the children of Esau fight against the children of Seir in former times, and the Lord had delivered the children of Seir into the hands of the children of Esau, and destroyed them from before them, and the children of Esau dwelt in their stead to this day.

(Jasher 84:6)
Therefore the Lord said to the children of Israel, Fight not against the children of Esau your brothers, for nothing in their land belongs to you, but you may buy food of them for money and eat it, and you may buy water of them for money and drink it.

(Jasher 84:7)
And the children of Israel did according to the word of the Lord.

(Jasher 84:8)
And the children of Israel went about the wilderness, going round by the way of Mount Sinai for a long time, and touched not the children of Esau, and they continued in that district for nineteen years.

(Jasher 84:9)
At that time died Latinus king of the children of Chittim, in the forty-fifth year of his reign, which is the fourteenth year of the children of Israel's departure from Egypt.

(Jasher 84:10)
And they buried him in his place which he had built for himself in the land of Chittim, and Abimnas reigned in his place for thirty-eight years.

(Jasher 84:11)
And the children of Israel passed the boundary of the children of Esau in those days, at the end of nineteen years, and they came and passed the road of the wilderness of Moab.

(Jasher 84:12)
And the Lord said to Moses, besiege not Moab, and do not fight against them, for I will give you nothing of their land.

(Jasher 84:13)
And the children of Israel passed the road of the wilderness of Moab for nineteen years, and they did not fight against them.

(Jasher 84:14)
And in the thirty-sixth year of the children of Israel's departing from Egypt the Lord smote the heart of Sihon, king of the Amorites, and he waged war, and went forth to fight against the children of Moab.

(Jasher 84:15)
And Sihon sent messengers to Beor the son of Janeas, the son of Balaam, counselor to the king of Egypt, and to Balaam his son, to curse Moab, in order that it might be delivered into the hand of Sihon.

(Jasher 84:16)
And the messengers went and brought Beor the son of Janeas, and Balaam his son, from Pethor in Mesopotamia, so Beor and Balaam his son came to the city of Sihon and they cursed

Moab and their king in the presence of Sihon king of the Amorites.

(Jasher 84:17)
So Sihon went out with his whole army, and he went to Moab and fought against them, and he subdued them, and the Lord delivered them into his hands, and Sihon slew the king of Moab.

(Jasher 84:18)
And Sihon took all the cities of Moab in the battle; he also took Heshbon from them, for Heshbon was one of the cities of Moab, and Sihon placed his princes and his nobles in Heshbon, and Heshbon belonged to Sihon in those days.

(Jasher 84:19)
Therefore the parable speakers Beor and Balaam his son uttered these words, saying, Come to Heshbon, the city of Sihon will be built and established.

(Jasher 84:20)
Woe to you Moab! You are lost, O people of Kemosh! Behold it is written upon the book of the law of God.

(Jasher 84:21)
And when Sihon had conquered Moab, he placed guards in the cities which he had taken from Moab, and a considerable number of the children of Moab fell in battle into the hand of Sihon, and he made a great capture of them, sons and daughters, and he slew their king; so Sihon turned back to his own land.

(Jasher 84:22)
And Sihon gave numerous presents of silver and gold to Beor and Balaam his son, and he dismissed them, and they went to

Mesopotamia to their home and country.

(Jasher 84:23)
At that time all the children of Israel passed from the road of the wilderness of Moab, and returned and surrounded the wilderness of Edom.

(Jasher 84:24)
So the whole congregation came to the wilderness of Sin in the first month of the fortieth year from their departure from Egypt, and the children of Israel dwelt there in Kadesh, of the wilderness of Sin, and Miriam died there and she was buried there.

(Numbers 20:14) (Jasher 84:25...)
And, at that time, Moses sent messengers from Kadesh to Hadad the king of Edom, saying, Thus says your brother Israel, you know all the travail that has befallen us:

(Numbers 20:15)
How our fathers went down into Egypt, and we have dwelt in Egypt a long time; and the Egyptians vexed us, and our fathers:

(Numbers 20:16)
And when we cried to the LORD, he heard our voice, and sent an angel, and has brought us forth out of Egypt: and, behold, we are in Kadesh, a city in the uttermost of your border:

(Numbers 20:17) (...Jasher 84:25)
Let us pass, I pray you, through your country: we will not pass through the fields, or through the vineyards, neither will we drink of the water of the wells: we will go by the king's high

way, we will not turn to the right hand nor to the left, until we have passed your borders.

(Numbers 20:18) (Jasher 84:26...)

And Edom said to him, You shall not pass by me through my country, lest I come out against you with the sword.

(Numbers 20:19)

And the children of Israel said to him, We will go by the high way: and if I and my cattle drink of your water, then I will pay for it: I will only, without doing any thing else, go through on my feet.

(Numbers 20:20) (...Jasher 84:26)

And he said, You shall not go through. And Edom came out against him and went forth to meet the children of Israel with much mighty people, and with a strong hand.

(Numbers 20:21) (Jasher 84:27)

Thus Edom refused to give Israel passage through his border: why Israel turned away from him and did not fight against them.

(Jasher 84:28)

For before this the Lord had commanded the children of Israel, saying, You shall not fight against the children of Esau, therefore the Israelites removed from them and did not fight against them.

(Numbers 20:22) (Jasher 84:29)

And the children of Israel, even the whole congregation, journeyed from Kadesh, and came to mount Hor.

(Numbers 20:23) (Jasher 84:30...)

And at that time, the LORD spoke to Moses and Aaron in mount Hor, by the coast of the land of Edom, saying,

(Numbers 20:24) (...Jasher 84:30)

Tell your brother Aaron that he shall die there, Aaron shall be gathered to his people: for he shall not enter into the land which I have given to the children of Israel, because you rebelled against my word at the water of Meribah.

(Numbers 20:25)

Take Aaron and Eleazar his son, and bring them up to mount Hor:

(Numbers 20:26)

And strip Aaron of his garments, and put them upon Eleazar his son: and Aaron shall be gathered to his people, and shall die there.

(Numbers 20:27)

And Moses did as the LORD commanded: and they went up into mount Hor in the sight of all the congregation.

(Jasher 84:31)

And Aaron went up, at the command of the Lord, to Mount Hor, in the fortieth year, in the fifth month, in the first day of the month.

(Numbers 20:28)

And Moses stripped Aaron of his garments, and put them upon Eleazar his son; and Aaron died there in the top of the mount: and Moses and Eleazar came down from the mount.

(Jasher 84:32)
And Aaron was one hundred and twenty-three years old when he died in Mount Hor

(Numbers 20:29)

And when all the congregation saw that Aaron was dead, they mourned for Aaron thirty days, even all the house of Israel.

Numbers: Chapter Twenty-One

(Numbers 21:1) (Jasher 85:1)
And when king Arad the Canaanite, which dwelt in the south, heard tell that Israel came by the way of the spies, and he arranged his forces to fight against the Israelites; then he fought against Israel, and took some of them prisoners.

(Jasher 85:2)
And the children of Israel were greatly afraid of him, for he had a great and heavy army, so the children of Israel resolved to return to Egypt.

(Jasher 85:3)
And the children of Israel turned back about the distance of three days' journey to Maserath Beni Jaakon, for they were greatly afraid on account of the king Arad.

(Jasher 85:4)
And the children of Israel would not get back to their places, so they remained in Beni Jaakon for thirty days.

(Jasher 85:5)
And when the children of Levi saw that the children of Israel would not turn back, they were jealous for the sake of the Lord, and they rose up and fought against the Israelites their brothers, and slew of them a great body, and forced them to turn back to their place, Mount Hor.

(Jasher 85:6)
And when they returned, king Arad was still arranging his

host for battle against the Israelites.

(Numbers 21:2) (Jasher 85:7)
And Israel vowed a vow to the LORD, and said, If you wilt indeed deliver this people into my hand, then I will utterly destroy their cities.

(Numbers 21:3) (Jasher 85:8)
And the LORD hearkened to the voice of Israel, and delivered up the Canaanites into their hand; and they utterly destroyed them and their cities: and he called the name of the place Hormah.

(Numbers 21:4) (Jasher 85:9...)
And they journeyed from mount Hor by the way of the Red sea, to compass the land of Edom: and the soul of the people was much discouraged because of the way.

(Numbers 21:5)
And the people spoke against God, and against Moses, Why have you brought us up out of Egypt to die in the wilderness? For there is no bread, neither is there any water; and our soul loathes this light bread.

(Numbers 21:6)
And the LORD sent fiery serpents among the people, and they bit the people; and much people of Israel died.

(Numbers 21:7)
Therefore the people came to Moses, and said, We have sinned, for we have spoken against the LORD, and against you; pray to the LORD, that he take away the serpents from us. And Moses prayed for the people.

(Numbers 21:8)

And the LORD said to Moses, Make you a fiery serpent, and set it upon a pole: and it shall come to pass, that every one that is bitten, when he looks upon it, shall live.

(Numbers 21:9)

And Moses made a serpent of brass, and put it upon a pole, and it came to pass, that if a serpent had bitten any man, when he beheld the serpent of brass, he lived.

(Numbers 21:10) (...Jasher 85:9...)

And the children of Israel set forward, and pitched in Oboth.

(Numbers 21:11) (...Jasher 85:9)

And they journeyed from Oboth, and pitched at Ijeabarim, in the wilderness which is before Moab, in the border of Moab, toward the sunrising.

(Jasher 85:10)

And the children of Israel sent to Moab, saying, Let us pass now through your land into our place, but the children of Moab would not suffer the children of Israel to pass through their land, for the children of Moab were greatly afraid lest the children of Israel should do to them as Sihon king of the Amorites had done to them, who had taken their land and had slain many of them.

(Jasher 85:11)

Therefore Moab would not suffer the Israelites to pass through his land, and the Lord commanded the children of Israel, saying, That they should not fight against Moab, so the Israelites removed from Moab.

(Jasher 85:12...)
And the children of Israel journeyed from the border of Moab.

(Numbers 21:12)
From there they removed, and pitched in the valley of Zared.

(Numbers 21:13) (...Jasher 85:12...)
From there they removed, and they came to and pitched on the other side of Arnon, which is in the wilderness that comes out of the coasts of the Amorites: for Arnon is the border of Moab, between Moab and the Amorites.

(Numbers 21:14)
Why it is said in the book of the wars of the LORD, What he did in the Red sea, and in the brooks of Arnon,

(Numbers 21:15)
And at the stream of the brooks that goes down to the dwelling of Ar, and lies upon the border of Moab.

(Numbers 21:16)
And from there they went to Beer: that is the well whereof the LORD spoke to Moses, Gather the people together, and I will give them water.

(Numbers 21:17)
Then Israel sang this song, Spring up, O well; sing you to it:

(Numbers 21:18)
The princes dug the well, the nobles of the people dug it, by the direction of the lawgiver, with their staves. And from the wilderness they went to Mattanah:

(Numbers 21:19)

And from Mattanah to Nahaliel: and from Nahaliel to Bamoth:

(Numbers 21:20)

And from Bamoth in the valley, that is in the country of Moab, to the top of Pisgah, which looks toward Jeshimon.

(...Jasher 85:12)

And they pitched in the border of Sihon, king of the Amorites, in the wilderness of Kedemoth.

(Numbers 21:21) (Jasher 85:13)

And the children of Israel sent messengers to Sihon king of the Amorites, saying,

(Numbers 21:22) (Jasher 85:14)

Let me pass through your land: we will not turn into the fields, or into the vineyards; we will not drink of the waters of the well: but we will go along by the king's high way, until we be past your borders.

(Numbers 21:23) (...Jasher 85:14, 15)

And Sihon would not suffer Israel to pass through his border: but Sihon gathered all his people together, and went out against Israel into the wilderness: and he came to Jahaz, and fought against Israel.

(Numbers 21:24...) (Jasher 85:16)

And the Lord delivered Sihon king of the Amorites into the hand of the children of Israel, and Israel smote him and all the people of Sihon with the edge of the sword and avenged the cause of Moab.

(...Numbers 21:24) (Jasher 85:17)

And the children of Israel possessed his land from Arnon to Jabbok, even to the children of Ammon: for the border of the children of Ammon was strong, and they took all the spoil of the cities.

(Numbers 21:25) (Jasher 85:18)

And Israel took all these cities: and Israel dwelt in all the cities of the Amorites, in Heshbon, and in all the villages thereof.

(Numbers 21:26)

For Heshbon was the city of Sihon the king of the Amorites, who had fought against the former king of Moab, and taken all his land out of his hand, even to Arnon.

(Numbers 21:27)

Why they that speak in proverbs say, Come into Heshbon, let the city of Sihon be built and prepared:

(Numbers 21:28)

For there is a fire gone out of Heshbon, a flame from the city of Sihon: it has consumed Ar of Moab, and the lords of the high places of Arnon.

(Numbers 21:29)

Woe to you, Moab! You are undone, O people of Chemosh: he has given his sons that escaped, and his daughters, into captivity to Sihon king of the Amorites.

(Numbers 21:30)

We have shot at them; Heshbon is perished even to Dibon, and we have laid them waste even to Nophah, which reaches to Medeba.

(Numbers 21:31)

Thus Israel dwelt in the land of the Amorites.

(Numbers 21:32)

And Moses sent to spy out Jaazer, and they took the villages thereof, and drove out the Amorites that were there.

(Jasher 85:19)
And all the children of Israel resolved to fight against the children of Ammon, to take their land also.

(Jasher 85:20)
So the Lord said to the children of Israel, Do not besiege the children of Ammon, neither stir up battle against them, for I will give nothing to you of their land, and the children of Israel hearkened to the word of the Lord, and did not fight against the children of Ammon.

(Numbers 21:33) (Jasher 85:21)

And they turned and went up by the way of Bashan to the land of Og, king of Bashan: and Og the king of Bashan went out against them to meet the Israelites in battle, he, and all his people, to the battle at Edrei. He had with him many valiant men, and a very strong force from the people of the Amorites.

(Jasher 85:22)
And Og king of Bashan was a very powerful man, but Naaron his son was exceedingly powerful, even stronger than he was.

(Jasher 85:23)
And Og said in his heart, Behold now the whole camp of Israel takes up a space of three parsa, now will I smite them at once without sword or spear.

(Jasher 85:24)
And Og went up Mount Jahaz, and took therefrom one large stone, the length of which was three parsa, and he placed it on his head, and resolved to throw it upon the camp of the children of Israel, to smite all the Israelites with that stone.

(Jasher 85:25)
And the angel of the Lord came and pierced the stone upon the head of Og, and the stone fell upon the neck of Og that Og fell to the earth on account of the weight of the stone upon his neck.

(Numbers 21:34) (Jasher 85:26)
And at that time, the LORD said to Moses and the children of Israel, Fear him not: for I have delivered him into your hand, and all his people, and his land; and you shall do to him as you did to Sihon king of the Amorites, which dwelt at Heshbon.

(Jasher 85:27)
And Moses went down to him with a small number of the children of Israel, and Moses smote Og with a stick at the ankles of his feet and slew him.

(Jasher 85:28)
The children of Israel afterward pursued the children of Og and all his people, and they beat and destroyed them till there was no remnant left of them.

(Numbers 21:35)
So they smote him, and his sons, and all his people, until there was none left him alive: and they possessed his land.

(Jasher 85:29)
Moses afterward sent some of the children of Israel to spy out

Jaazer, for Jaazer was a very famous city.

(Jasher 85:30)
And the spies went to Jaazer and explored it, and the spies trusted in the Lord, and they fought against the men of Jaazer.

(Jasher 85:31)
And these men took Jaazer and its villages, and the Lord delivered them into their hand, and they drove out the Amorites who had been there.

(Jasher 85:32)
And the children of Israel took the land of the two kings of the Amorites, sixty cities which were on the other side of Jordan, from the brook of Arnon to Mount Herman.

Numbers: Chapter Twenty-Two

(Numbers 22:1) (Jasher 85:33)

And the children of Israel set forward, journeyed and came into the plain of Moab, and pitched in the plains of Moab which is on this side Jordan by Jericho.

(Numbers 22:2)

And Balak the son of Zippor saw all that Israel had done to the Amorites.

(Numbers 22:3) (Jasher 85:34)

And the children of Moab heard all the evil which the children of Israel had done to the two kings of the Amorites, to Sihon and Og, so all the men of Moab were sore afraid of the people, because they were many: and Moab was distressed because of the children of Israel.

(Jasher 85:35)

And the elders of Moab said, Behold the two kings of the Amorites, Sihon and Og, who were more powerful than all the kings of the earth, could not stand against the children of Israel, how then can we stand before them?

(Jasher 85:36)

Surely they sent us a message before now to pass through our land on their way, and we would not suffer them, now they will turn upon us with their heavy swords and destroy us; and Moab was distressed on account of the children of Israel, and they were greatly afraid of them, and they counseled together what was to be done to the children of Israel.

(Jasher 85:37)
And the elders of Moab resolved and took one of their men, Balak the son of Zippor the Moabite, and made him king over them at that time, and Balak was a very wise man.

(Jasher 85:38)
And the elders of Moab rose up and sent to the children of Midian to make peace with them, for a great battle and enmity had been in those days between Moab and Midian, from the days of Hadad the son of Bedad king of Edom, who smote Midian in the field of Moab, to these days.

(Jasher 85:39)
And the children of Moab sent to the children of Midian, and they made peace with them, and the elders of Midian came to the land of Moab to make peace in behalf of the children of Midian.

(Jasher 85:40)
And the elders of Moab counseled with the elders of Midian what to do in order to save their lives from Israel.

(Numbers 22:4) (Jasher 85:41)
And all the children of Moab said to the elders of Midian, Now shall this company, the children of Israel, lick up all that are round about us, as the ox licks up the grass of the field, for thus did they do to the two kings of the Amorites who are stronger than we are. And Balak the son of Zippor was king of the Moabites at that time.

(Jasher 85:42)
And the elders of Midian said to Moab, We have heard that

at the time when Sihon king of the Amorites fought against you, when he prevailed over you and took your land, he had sent to Beor the son of Janeas and to Balaam his son from Mesopotamia, and they came and cursed you; therefore did the hand of Sihon prevail over you, that he took your land.

(Jasher 85:43)
Now therefore send you also to Balaam his son, for he still remains in his land, and give him his hire, that he may come and curse all the people of whom you are afraid; so the elders of Moab heard this thing, and it pleased them to send to Balaam the son of Beor.

(Numbers 22:5) (Jasher 85:44, 45)
So Balak the son of Zippor king of Moab sent messengers therefore to Balaam the son of Beor to Pethor, which is by the river of the land of the children of his people, to call him, saying, Behold, there is a people come out from Egypt: behold, they cover the face of the earth, and they abide over against me:

(Numbers 22:6) (Jasher 85:46)
Come now therefore, I pray you, curse this people for me; for they are too mighty for me: peradventure I shall prevail to fight against them, that we may smite them, and that I may drive them out of the land: for I heard that he whom you bless is blessed, and he whom you curse is cursed.

(Numbers 22:7) (Jasher 85:47...)
And the messengers of Balak, the elders of Moab and the elders of Midian, departed with the rewards of divination in their hand, and went to Balaam; and they came to Balaam, and spoke to him the words of Balak.

(Numbers 22:8)

And he said to them, Lodge here this night, and I will bring you word again, as the LORD shall speak to me: and the princes of Moab abode with Balaam.

(Numbers 22:9)

And God came to Balaam, and said, What men are these with you?

(Numbers 22:10)

And Balaam said to God, Balak the son of Zippor, king of Moab, has sent to me, saying,

(Numbers 22:11)

Behold, there is a people come out of Egypt, which covers the face of the earth: come now, curse me them; peradventure I shall be able to overcome them, and drive them out.

(Numbers 22:12)

And God said to Balaam, You shall not go with them; you shall not curse the people: for they are blessed.

(Numbers 22:13)

And Balaam rose up in the morning, and said to the princes of Balak, Get you into your land: for the LORD refuses to give me leave to go with you.

(Numbers 22:14)

And the princes of Moab rose up, and they went to Balak, and said, Balaam refuses to come with us.

(Numbers 22:15)

And Balak sent yet again princes, more, and more honorable than they.

(Numbers 22:16)

And they came to Balaam, and said to him, Thus says Balak the son of Zippor, Let nothing, I pray you, hinder you from coming to me:

(Numbers 22:17)

For I will promote you to very great honor, and I will do whatsoever you say to me: come therefore, I pray you, curse me this people.

(Numbers 22:18)

And Balaam answered and said to the servants of Balak, If Balak would give me his house full of silver and gold, I cannot go beyond the word of the LORD my God, to do less or more.

(Numbers 22:19)

Now therefore, I pray you, tarry you also here this night, that I may know what the LORD will say to me more.

(Numbers 22:20)

And God came to Balaam at night, and said to him, If the men come to call you, rise up, and go with them; but yet the word which I shall say to you, that shall you do.

(Numbers 22:21)

And Balaam rose up in the morning, and saddled his donkey, and went with the princes of Moab.

(Numbers 22:22)

And God's anger was kindled because he went: and the angel of the LORD stood in the way for an adversary against him. Now he was riding upon his donkey, and his two servants were with him.

(Numbers 22:23)
And the donkey saw the angel of the LORD standing in the way, and his sword drawn in his hand: and the donkey turned aside out of the way, and went into the field: and Balaam smote the donkey, to turn her into the way.

(Numbers 22:24)
But the angel of the LORD stood in a path of the vineyards, a wall being on this side, and a wall on that side.

(Numbers 22:25)
And when the donkey saw the angel of the LORD, she thrust herself to the wall, and crushed Balaam's foot against the wall: and he smote her again.

(Numbers 22:26)
And the angel of the LORD went further, and stood in a narrow place, where was no way to turn either to the right hand or to the left.

(Numbers 22:27)
And when the donkey saw the angel of the LORD, she fell down under Balaam: and Balaam's anger was kindled, and he smote the donkey with a staff.

(Numbers 22:28)
And the LORD opened the mouth of the donkey, and she said to Balaam, What have I done to you, that you have smitten me these three times?

(Numbers 22:29)
And Balaam said to the donkey, Because you have mocked me: I would there were a sword in mine hand, for now would I kill you.

(Numbers 22:30)
And the donkey said to Balaam, Am not I your donkey, upon which you have ridden ever since I was yours to this day? Was I ever wont to do so to you? And he said, Nay.

(Numbers 22:31)
Then the LORD opened the eyes of Balaam, and he saw the angel of the LORD standing in the way, and his sword drawn in his hand: and he bowed down his head, and fell flat on his face.

(Numbers 22:32)
And the angel of the LORD said to him, Why have you smitten your donkey these three times? Behold, I went out to withstand you, because your way is perverse before me:

(Numbers 22:33)
And the donkey saw me, and turned from me these three times: unless she had turned from me, surely now also I had slain you, and saved her alive.

(Numbers 22:34)
And Balaam said to the angel of the LORD, I have sinned; for I knew not that you stood in the way against me: now therefore, if it displease you, I will get me back again.

(Numbers 22:35)
And the angel of the LORD said to Balaam, Go with the men: but only the word that I shall speak to you, that you shall speak. So Balaam went with the princes of Balak.

(...Jasher 85:47)
And they brought Balaam to curse the people to fight against Moab.

(Numbers 22:36)

And when Balak heard that Balaam was come, he went out to meet him to a city of Moab, which is in the border of Arnon, which is in the utmost coast.

(Jasher 85:48)

And Balaam came to Balak to curse Israel, and the Lord said to Balaam, Curse not this people for it is blessed.

(Numbers 22:37)

And Balak said to Balaam, Did I not earnestly send to you to call you? Why did you come not to me? Am I not able indeed to promote you to honor?

(Numbers 22:38)

And Balaam said to Balak, Lo, I am come to you: have I now any power at all to say any thing? The word that God puts in my mouth, that shall I speak.

(Numbers 22:39)

And Balaam went with Balak, and they came to Kirjathhuzoth.

(Numbers 22:40)

And Balak offered oxen and sheep, and sent to Balaam, and to the princes that were with him.

(Numbers 22:41)

And it came to pass on the morrow, that Balak took Balaam, and brought him up into the high places of Baal, that there he might see the utmost part of the people.

Numbers: Chapter Twenty-Three

(Numbers 23:1)
And Balaam said to Balak, Build me here seven altars, and prepare me here seven oxen and seven rams.

(Numbers 23:2)
And Balak did as Balaam had spoken; and Balak and Balaam offered on every altar a bullock and a ram.

(Numbers 23:3)
And Balaam said to Balak, Stand by your burnt offering, and I will go: peradventure the LORD will come to meet me: and whatsoever he shows me I will tell you. And he went to an high place.

(Numbers 23:4)
And God met Balaam: and he said to him, I have prepared seven altars, and I have offered upon every altar a bullock and a ram.

(Numbers 23:5)
And the LORD put a word in Balaam's mouth, and said, Return to Balak, and thus you shall speak.

(Numbers 23:6)
And he returned to him, and, lo, he stood by his burnt sacrifice, he, and all the princes of Moab.

(Numbers 23:7)
And he took up his parable, and said, Balak the king of Moab

has brought me from Aram, out of the mountains of the east, saying, Come, curse me Jacob, and come, defy Israel.

(Numbers 23:8)
How shall I curse, whom God has not cursed? Or how shall I defy, whom the LORD has not defied?

(Numbers 23:9)
For from the top of the rocks I see him, and from the hills I behold him: lo, the people shall dwell alone, and shall not be reckoned among the nations.

(Numbers 23:10)
Who can count the dust of Jacob, and the number of the fourth part of Israel? Let me die the death of the righteous, and let my last end be like his!

(Numbers 23:11)
And Balak said to Balaam, What have you done to me? I took you to curse mine enemies, and, behold, you have blessed them altogether.

(Numbers 23:12)
And he answered and said, Must I not take heed to speak that which the LORD has put in my mouth?

(Jasher 85:49)
And Balak urged Balaam day by day to curse Israel, but Balaam hearkened not to Balak on account of the word of the Lord which he had spoken to Balaam.

(Numbers 23:13)
And Balak said to him, Come, I pray you, with me to another place, from where you may see them: you shall see but the

utmost part of them, and shall not see them all: and curse me them from there.

(Numbers 23:14)
And he brought him into the field of Zophim, to the top of Pisgah, and built seven altars, and offered a bullock and a ram on every altar.

(Numbers 23:15)
And he said to Balak, Stand here by your burnt offering, while I meet the LORD yonder.

(Numbers 23:16)
And the LORD met Balaam, and put a word in his mouth, and said, Go again to Balak, and say thus.

(Numbers 23:17)
And when he came to him, behold, he stood by his burnt offering, and the princes of Moab with him. And Balak said to him, What has the LORD spoken?

(Numbers 23:18)
And he took up his parable, and said, Rise up, Balak, and hear; hearken to me, you son of Zippor:

(Numbers 23:19)
God is not a man, that he should lie; neither the son of man, that he should repent: has he said, and shall he not do it? Or has he spoken, and shall he not make it good?

(Numbers 23:20)
Behold, I have received commandment to bless: and he has blessed; and I cannot reverse it.

(Numbers 23:21)

He has not beheld iniquity in Jacob, neither has he seen perverseness in Israel: the LORD his God is with him, and the shout of a king is among them.

(Numbers 23:22)

God brought them out of Egypt; he has as it were the strength of an unicorn.

(Numbers 23:23)

Surely there is no enchantment against Jacob, neither is there any divination against Israel: according to this time it shall be said of Jacob and of Israel, What has God wrought!

(Numbers 23:24)

Behold, the people shall rise up as a great lion, and lift up himself as a young lion: he shall not lie down until he eat of the prey, and drink the blood of the slain.

(Numbers 23:25)

And Balak said to Balaam, Neither curse them at all, nor bless them at all.

(Numbers 23:26)

But Balaam answered and said to Balak, Told not I you, saying, All that the LORD speaks, that I must do?

(Numbers 23:27)

And Balak said to Balaam, Come, I pray you, I will bring you to another place; peradventure it will please God that you may curse me them from there.

(Numbers 23:28)

And Balak brought Balaam to the top of Peor, that looks toward Jeshimon.

(Numbers 23:29)

And Balaam said to Balak, Build me here seven altars, and prepare me here seven bullocks and seven rams.

(Numbers 23:30)

And Balak did as Balaam had said, and offered a bullock and a ram on every altar.

Numbers: Chapter Twenty-Four

(Numbers 24:1)
And when Balaam saw that it pleased the LORD to bless Israel, he went not, as at other times, to seek for enchantments, but he set his face toward the wilderness.

(Numbers 24:2)
And Balaam lifted up his eyes, and he saw Israel abiding in his tents according to their tribes; and the spirit of God came upon him.

(Numbers 24:3)
And he took up his parable, and said, Balaam the son of Beor has said, and the man whose eyes are open has said:

(Numbers 24:4)
He has said, which heard the words of God, which saw the vision of the Almighty, falling into a trance, but having his eyes open:

(Numbers 24:5)
How goodly are your tents, O Jacob, and your tabernacles, O Israel!

(Numbers 24:6)
As the valleys are they spread forth, as gardens by the river's side, as the trees of lign aloes which the LORD has planted, and as cedar trees beside the waters.

(Numbers 24:7)

He shall pour the water out of his buckets, and his seed shall be in many waters, and his king shall be higher than Agag, and his kingdom shall be exalted.

(Numbers 24:8)

God brought him forth out of Egypt; he has as it were the strength of an unicorn: he shall eat up the nations his enemies, and shall break their bones, and pierce them through with his arrows.

(Numbers 24:9)

He couched, he lay down as a lion, and as a great lion: who shall stir him up? Blessed is he that blesses you, and cursed is he that curses you.

(Numbers 24:10)

And Balak's anger was kindled against Balaam, and he smote his hands together: and Balak said to Balaam, I called you to curse mine enemies, and, behold, you have altogether blessed them these three times.

(Numbers 24:11)

Therefore now flee to your place: I thought to promote you to great honor; but, lo, the LORD has kept you back from honor.

(Numbers 24:12)

And Balaam said to Balak, Spoke I not also to your messengers which you sent to me, saying,

(Numbers 24:13)

If Balak would give me his house full of silver and gold, I cannot go beyond the commandment of the LORD, to do either good or bad of mine own mind; but what the LORD says, that will I speak?

(Numbers 24:14)
And now, behold, I go to my people: come therefore, and I will advertise you what this people shall do to your people in the latter days.

(Numbers 24:15)
And he took up his parable, and said, Balaam the son of Beor has said, and the man whose eyes are open has said:

(Numbers 24:16)
He has said, which heard the words of God, and knew the knowledge of the most High, which saw the vision of the Almighty, falling into a trance, but having his eyes open:

(Numbers 24:17)
I shall see him, but not now: I shall behold him, but not nigh: there shall come a Star out of Jacob, and a Scepter shall rise out of Israel, and shall smite the corners of Moab, and destroy all the children of Sheth.

(Numbers 24:18)
And Edom shall be a possession, Seir also shall be a possession for his enemies; and Israel shall do valiantly.

(Numbers 24:19)
Out of Jacob shall come he that shall have dominion, and shall destroy him that remains of the city.

(Numbers 24:20)
And when he looked on Amalek, he took up his parable, and said, Amalek was the first of the nations; but his latter end shall be that he perish forever.

(Numbers 24:21)

And he looked on the Kenites, and took up his parable, and said, Strong is your dwelling place, and you put your nest in a rock.

(Numbers 24:22)

Nevertheless the Kenite shall be wasted, until Asshur shall carry you away captive.

(Numbers 24:23)

And he took up his parable, and said, Alas, who shall live when God does this!

(Numbers 24:24)

And ships shall come from the coast of Chittim, and shall afflict Asshur, and shall afflict Eber, and he also shall perish forever.

(Numbers 24:25) (Jasher 85:50)

And Balaam rose up, and returned to his land and went from there to Midian and returned to his place: and when Balak saw that Balaam would not accede to his wish, he also rose up and went his way home.

Numbers: Chapter Twenty-Five

(Jasher 85:51)
And the children of Israel journeyed from the plain of Moab, and pitched by Jordan from Beth-jesimoth even to Abel-shittim, at the end of the plains of Moab.

(Numbers 25:1) (Jasher 85:52)
And the children of Israel abode in the plain of Shittim, and the people began to commit whoredom with the daughters of Moab.

(Jasher 85:53)
And the children of Israel approached Moab, and the children of Moab pitched their tents opposite to the camp of the children of Israel.

(Jasher 85:54)
And the children of Moab were afraid of the children of Israel, and the children of Moab took all their daughters and their wives of beautiful aspect and comely appearance, and dressed them in gold and silver and costly garments.

(Jasher 85:55)
And the children of Moab seated those women at the door of their tents, in order that the children of Israel might see them and turn to them, and not fight against Moab.

(Jasher 85:56)
And all the children of Moab did this thing to the children of Israel, and every man placed his wife and daughter at the

door of his tent, and all the children of Israel saw the act of the children of Moab, and the children of Israel turned to the daughters of Moab and coveted them, and they went to them.

(Jasher 85:57)
And it came to pass that when a Hebrew came to the door of the tent of Moab, and saw a daughter of Moab and desired her in his heart, and spoke with her at the door of the tent that which he desired, while they were speaking together the men of the tent would come out and speak to the Hebrew like to these words:

(Jasher 85:58)
Surely you know that we are brothers, we are all the descendants of Lot and the descendants of Abraham his brother, why then will you not remain with us, and why will you not eat our bread and our sacrifice?

(Jasher 85:59)
And when the children of Moab had thus overwhelmed him with their speeches, and enticed him by their flattering words, they seated him in the tent and cooked and sacrificed for him, and he ate of their sacrifice and of their bread.

(Jasher 85:60)
They then gave him wine and he drank and became intoxicated, and they placed before him a beautiful damsel, and he did with her as he liked, for he knew not what he was doing, as he had drunk plentifully of wine.

(Numbers 25:2)
And they called the people to the sacrifices of their gods: and the people did eat, and bowed down to their gods.

(Numbers 25:3) (Jasher 85:61)

Thus did the children of Moab to Israel in that place, in the plain of Shittim. And Israel joined himself to Baalpeor: and the anger of the LORD was kindled against Israel on account of this matter, and he sent a pestilence among them, and there died of the Israelites twenty-four thousand men.

(Numbers 25:4)

And the LORD said to Moses, Take all the heads of the people, and hang them up before the LORD against the sun, that the fierce anger of the LORD may be turned away from Israel.

(Numbers 25:5)

And Moses said to the judges of Israel, Slay you every one his men that were joined to Baalpeor.

(Numbers 25:6) (Jasher 85:62...)

And, behold, now there was a man, one of the children of Israel, who came and brought to his brethren, and connected himself with the Midianite woman, in the sight of Moses, and in the sight of all the congregation of the children of Israel, who were weeping before the door of the tabernacle of the congregation.

(Numbers 25:7) (Jasher 85:63...)

And when Phinehas, the son of Eleazar, the son of Aaron the priest, saw it, this wicked thing which Zimri had done, he rose up from among the congregation, and took a javelin in his hand;

(Numbers 25:8) (...Jasher 85:63)

And he went after the man of Israel into the tent, and thrust both of them through, the man of Israel, and the woman through her belly, and slew them. So the plague was stayed from the children of Israel.

(Numbers 25:9)
And those that died in the plague were twenty and four thousand.

(Numbers 25:10)
And the LORD spoke to Moses, saying,

(Numbers 25:11)
Phinehas, the son of Eleazar, the son of Aaron the priest, has turned my wrath away from the children of Israel, while he was zealous for my sake among them, that I consumed not the children of Israel in my jealousy.

(Numbers 25:12)
Why say, Behold, I give to him my covenant of peace:

(Numbers 25:13)
And he shall have it, and his seed after him, even the covenant of an everlasting priesthood; because he was zealous for his God, and made an atonement for the children of Israel.

(Numbers 25:14) (...Jasher 85:62...)
Now the name of the Israelite that was slain, even that was slain with the Midianitish woman, was of Simeon whose name was Zimri, the son of Salu, a prince of a chief house among the Simeonites.

(Numbers 25:15) (...Jasher 85:62)
And the name of the Midianite woman that was slain was Cozbi, the daughter of Zur, king of Midian; he was head over a people, and of a chief house in Midian.

(Numbers 25:16)

And the LORD spoke to Moses, saying,

(Numbers 25:17)

Vex the Midianites, and smite them:

(Numbers 25:18)

For they vex you with their wiles, wherewith they have beguiled you in the matter of Peor, and in the matter of Cozbi, the daughter of a prince of Midian, their sister, which was slain in the day of the plague for Peor's sake.

Numbers: Chapter Twenty-Six

(Numbers 26:1) (Jasher 86:1)

And at that time, it came to pass after the plague, that the LORD spoke to Moses and to Eleazar the son of Aaron the priest, saying,

(Numbers 26:2) (Jasher 86:2)

Take the sum of the heads of all the congregation of the children of Israel, from twenty years old and upward, throughout their fathers' house, all that went forth in the army and are able to go to war in Israel.

(Numbers 26:3)

And Moses and Eleazar the priest spoke with them in the plains of Moab by Jordan near Jericho, saying,

(Numbers 26:4)

Take the sum of the people, from twenty years old and upward; as the LORD commanded Moses and the children of Israel, which went forth out of the land of Egypt.

(Numbers 26:5)

Reuben, the eldest son of Israel: the children of Reuben; Hanoch, of whom comes the family of the Hanochites: of Pallu, the family of the Palluites:

(Numbers 26:6)

Of Hezron, the family of the Hezronites: of Carmi, the family of the Carmites.

(Numbers 26:7)

These are the families of the Reubenites: and they that were numbered of them were forty and three thousand and seven hundred and thirty.

(Numbers 26:8)

And the sons of Pallu; Eliab.

(Numbers 26:9)

And the sons of Eliab; Nemuel, and Dathan, and Abiram. This is that Dathan and Abiram, which were famous in the congregation, who strove against Moses and against Aaron in the company of Korah, when they strove against the LORD:

(Numbers 26:10)

And the earth opened her mouth, and swallowed them up together with Korah, when that company died, what time the fire devoured two hundred and fifty men: and they became a sign.

(Numbers 26:11)

Notwithstanding the children of Korah died not.

(Numbers 26:12)

The sons of Simeon after their families: of Nemuel, the family of the Nemuelites: of Jamin, the family of the Jaminites: of Jachin, the family of the Jachinites:

(Numbers 26:13)

Of Zerah, the family of the Zarhites: of Shaul, the family of the Shaulites.

(Numbers 26:14)

These are the families of the Simeonites, twenty and two

thousand and two hundred.

(Numbers 26:15)
The children of Gad after their families: of Zephon, the family of the Zephonites: of Haggi, the family of the Haggites: of Shuni, the family of the Shunites:

(Numbers 26:16)
Of Ozni, the family of the Oznites: of Eri, the family of the Erites:

(Numbers 26:17)
Of Arod, the family of the Arodites: of Areli, the family of the Arelites.

(Numbers 26:18)
These are the families of the children of Gad according to those that were numbered of them, forty thousand and five hundred.

(Numbers 26:19)
The sons of Judah were Er and Onan: and Er and Onan died in the land of Canaan.

(Numbers 26:20)
And the sons of Judah after their families were; of Shelah, the family of the Shelanites: of Pharez, the family of the Pharzites: of Zerah, the family of the Zarhites.

(Numbers 26:21)
And the sons of Pharez were; of Hezron, the family of the Hezronites: of Hamul, the family of the Hamulites.

(Numbers 26:22)
These are the families of Judah according to those that were numbered of them, threescore and sixteen thousand and five hundred.

(Numbers 26:23)
Of the sons of Issachar after their families: of Tola, the family of the Tolaites: of Pua, the family of the Punites:

(Numbers 26:24)
Of Jashub, the family of the Jashubites: of Shimron, the family of the Shimronites.

(Numbers 26:25)
These are the families of Issachar according to those that were numbered of them, threescore and four thousand and three hundred.

(Numbers 26:26)
Of the sons of Zebulun after their families: of Sered, the family of the Sardites: of Elon, the family of the Elonites: of Jahleel, the family of the Jahleelites.

(Numbers 26:27)
These are the families of the Zebulunites according to those that were numbered of them, threescore thousand and five hundred.

(Numbers 26:28)
The sons of Joseph after their families were Manasseh and Ephraim.

(Numbers 26:29)
Of the sons of Manasseh: of Machir, the family of the

Machirites: and Machir begot Gilead: of Gilead come the family of the Gileadites.

(Numbers 26:30)
These are the sons of Gilead: of Jeezer, the family of the Jeezerites: of Helek, the family of the Helekites:

(Numbers 26:31)
And of Asriel, the family of the Asrielites: and of Shechem, the family of the Shechemites:

(Numbers 26:32)
And of Shemida, the family of the Shemidaites: and of Hepher, the family of the Hepherites.

(Numbers 26:33)
And Zelophehad the son of Hepher had no sons, but daughters: and the names of the daughters of Zelophehad were Mahlah, and Noah, Hoglah, Milcah, and Tirzah.

(Numbers 26:34)
These are the families of Manasseh, and those that were numbered of them, fifty and two thousand and seven hundred.

(Numbers 26:35)
These are the sons of Ephraim after their families: of Shuthelah, the family of the Shuthalhites: of Becher, the family of the Bachrites: of Tahan, the family of the Tahanites.

(Numbers 26:36)
And these are the sons of Shuthelah: of Eran, the family of the Eranites.

(Numbers 26:37)

These are the families of the sons of Ephraim according to those that were numbered of them, thirty and two thousand and five hundred. These are the sons of Joseph after their families.

(Numbers 26:38)

The sons of Benjamin after their families: of Bela, the family of the Belaites: of Ashbel, the family of the Ashbelites: of Ahiram, the family of the Ahiramites:

(Numbers 26:39)

Of Shupham, the family of the Shuphamites: of Hupham, the family of the Huphamites.

(Numbers 26:40)

And the sons of Bela were Ard and Naaman: of Ard, the family of the Ardites: and of Naaman, the family of the Naamites.

(Numbers 26:41)

These are the sons of Benjamin after their families: and they that were numbered of them were forty and five thousand and six hundred.

(Numbers 26:42)

These are the sons of Dan after their families: of Shuham, the family of the Shuhamites. These are the families of Dan after their families.

(Numbers 26:43)

All the families of the Shuhamites, according to those that were numbered of them, were threescore and four thousand and four hundred.

(Numbers 26:44)

Of the children of Asher after their families: of Jimna, the family of the Jimnites: of Jesui, the family of the Jesuites: of Beriah, the family of the Beriites.

(Numbers 26:45)

Of the sons of Beriah: of Heber, the family of the Heberites: of Malchiel, the family of the Malchielites.

(Numbers 26:46)

And the name of the daughter of Asher was Sarah.

(Numbers 26:47)

These are the families of the sons of Asher according to those that were numbered of them; who were fifty and three thousand and four hundred.

(Numbers 26:48)

Of the sons of Naphtali after their families: of Jahzeel, the family of the Jahzeelites: of Guni, the family of the Gunites:

(Numbers 26:49)

Of Jezer, the family of the Jezerites: of Shillem, the family of the Shillemites.

(Numbers 26:50)

These are the families of Naphtali according to their families: and they that were numbered of them were forty and five thousand and four hundred.

(Numbers 26:51)

These were the numbered of the children of Israel, six hundred thousand and a thousand seven hundred and thirty.

(Jasher 86:3...)
And the number of all Israel was seven hundred thousand, seven hundred and thirty.

(Numbers 26:52)
And the LORD spoke to Moses, saying,

(Numbers 26:53)
To these the land shall be divided for an inheritance according to the number of names.

(Numbers 26:54)
To many you shall give the more inheritance, and to few you shall give the less inheritance: to every one shall his inheritance be given according to those that were numbered of him.

(Numbers 26:55)
Notwithstanding the land shall be divided by lot: according to the names of the tribes of their fathers they shall inherit.

(Numbers 26:56)
According to the lot shall the possession thereof be divided between many and few.

(Numbers 26:57)
And these are they that were numbered of the Levites after their families: of Gershon, the family of the Gershonites: of Kohath, the family of the Kohathites: of Merari, the family of the Merarites.

(Numbers 26:58)
These are the families of the Levites: the family of the Libnites, the family of the Hebronites, the family of the Mahlites, the

family of the Mushites, the family of the Korathites. And Kohath begot Amram.

(Numbers 26:59)

And the name of Amram's wife was Jochebed, the daughter of Levi, whom her mother bare to Levi in Egypt: and she bare to Amram Aaron and Moses, and Miriam their sister.

(Numbers 26:60)

And to Aaron was born Nadab, and Abihu, Eleazar, and Ithamar.

(Numbers 26:61)

And Nadab and Abihu died, when they offered strange fire before the LORD.

(Numbers 26:62) (Jasher 86:4...)

And those that were numbered of them, of the children of Levi, were twenty and three thousand, all males from a month old and upward: for they were not numbered among the children of Israel, because there was no inheritance given them among the children of Israel.

(Numbers 26:63) (...Jasher 86:3)

These are they that were numbered by Moses and Eleazar the priest, who numbered the children of Israel after their families, in the plains of Moab by Jordan near Jericho.

(Numbers 26:64) (...Jasher 86:4)

But among these there was not a man of them whom Moses and Aaron the priest numbered, when they numbered the children of Israel in the wilderness of Sinai.

(Numbers 26:65) (Jasher 86:5)

For the LORD had said of them, They shall surely die in the wilderness. So they all died, And there was not left a man of them, save Caleb the son of Jephunneh, and Joshua the son of Nun.

Numbers: Chapter Twenty-Seven

(Numbers 27:1)

Then came the daughters of Zelophehad, the son of Hepher, the son of Gilead, the son of Machir, the son of Manasseh, of the families of Manasseh the son of Joseph: and these are the names of his daughters; Mahlah, Noah, and Hoglah, and Milcah, and Tirzah.

(Numbers 27:2)

And they stood before Moses, and before Eleazar the priest, and before the princes and all the congregation, by the door of the tabernacle of the congregation, saying,

(Numbers 27:3)

Our father died in the wilderness, and he was not in the company of them that gathered themselves together against the LORD in the company of Korah; but died in his own sin, and had no sons.

(Numbers 27:4)

Why should the name of our father be done away from among his family, because he has no son? Give to us therefore a possession among the brethren of our father.

(Numbers 27:5)

And Moses brought their cause before the LORD.

(Numbers 27:6)

And the LORD spoke to Moses, saying,

(Numbers 27:7)

The daughters of Zelophehad speak right: you shall surely give them a possession of an inheritance among their father's brethren; and you shall cause the inheritance of their father to pass to them.

(Numbers 27:8)

And you shall speak to the children of Israel, saying, If a man die, and have no son, then you shall cause his inheritance to pass to his daughter.

(Numbers 27:9)

And if he have no daughter, then you shall give his inheritance to his brethren.

(Numbers 27:10)

And if he have no brethren, then you shall give his inheritance to his father's brethren.

(Numbers 27:11)

And if his father have no brethren, then you shall give his inheritance to his kinsman that is next to him of his family, and he shall possess it: and it shall be to the children of Israel a statute of judgment, as the LORD commanded Moses.

(Numbers 27:12)

And the LORD said to Moses, Get you up into this mount Abarim, and see the land which I have given to the children of Israel.

(Numbers 27:13)

And when you have seen it, you also shall be gathered to your people, as Aaron your brother was gathered.

(Numbers 27:14)

For you rebelled against my commandment in the desert of Zin, in the strife of the congregation, to sanctify me at the water before their eyes: that is the water of Meribah in Kadesh in the wilderness of Zin.

(Numbers 27:15)

And Moses spoke to the LORD, saying,

(Numbers 27:16)

Let the LORD, the God of the spirits of all flesh, set a man over the congregation,

(Numbers 27:17)

Which may go out before them, and which may go in before them, and which may lead them out, and which may bring them in; that the congregation of the LORD be not as sheep which have no shepherd.

(Numbers 27:18)

And the LORD said to Moses, Take you Joshua the son of Nun, a man in whom is the spirit, and lay your hand upon him;

(Numbers 27:19)

And set him before Eleazar the priest, and before all the congregation; and give him a charge in their sight.

(Numbers 27:20)

And you shall put some of your honor upon him, that all the congregation of the children of Israel may be obedient.

(Numbers 27:21)

And he shall stand before Eleazar the priest, who shall ask counsel for him after the judgment of Urim before the LORD:

at his word shall they go out, and at his word they shall come in, both he, and all the children of Israel with him, even all the congregation.

(Numbers 27:22)
And Moses did as the LORD commanded him: and he took Joshua, and set him before Eleazar the priest, and before all the congregation:

(Numbers 27:23)
And he laid his hands upon him, and gave him a charge, as the LORD commanded by the hand of Moses.

Numbers: Chapter Twenty-Eight

(Numbers 28:1)
And the LORD spoke to Moses, saying,

(Numbers 28:2)
Command the children of Israel, and say to them, My offering, and my bread for my sacrifices made by fire, for a sweet savor to me, shall you observe to offer to me in their due season.

(Numbers 28:3)
And you shall say to them, This is the offering made by fire which you shall offer to the LORD; two lambs of the first year without spot day by day, for a continual burnt offering.

(Numbers 28:4)
The one lamb shall you offer in the morning, and the other lamb shall you offer at even;

(Numbers 28:5)
And a tenth part of an ephah of flour for a meat offering, mingled with the fourth part of a hin of beaten oil.

(Numbers 28:6)
It is a continual burnt offering, which was ordained in mount Sinai for a sweet savor, a sacrifice made by fire to the LORD.

(Numbers 28:7)
And the drink offering thereof shall be the fourth part of a hin for the one lamb: in the holy place shall you cause the strong wine to be poured to the LORD for a drink offering.

(Numbers 28:8)

And the other lamb shall you offer at even: as the meat offering of the morning, and as the drink offering thereof, you shall offer it, a sacrifice made by fire, of a sweet savor to the LORD.

(Numbers 28:9)

And on the sabbath day two lambs of the first year without spot, and two tenth deals of flour for a meat offering, mingled with oil, and the drink offering thereof:

(Numbers 28:10)

This is the burnt offering of every sabbath, beside the continual burnt offering, and his drink offering.

(Numbers 28:11)

And in the beginnings of your months you shall offer a burnt offering to the LORD; two young bullocks, and one ram, seven lambs of the first year without spot;

(Numbers 28:12)

And three tenth deals of flour for a meat offering, mingled with oil, for one bullock; and two tenth deals of flour for a meat offering, mingled with oil, for one ram;

(Numbers 28:13)

And a several tenth deal of flour mingled with oil for a meat offering to one lamb; for a burnt offering of a sweet savor, a sacrifice made by fire to the LORD.

(Numbers 28:14)

And their drink offerings shall be half a hin of wine to a bullock, and the third part of a hin to a ram, and a fourth part of a hin to a lamb: this is the burnt offering of every month throughout the months of the year.

(Numbers 28:15)
And one kid of the goats for a sin offering to the LORD shall be offered, beside the continual burnt offering, and his drink offering.

(Numbers 28:16)
And in the fourteenth day of the first month is the passover of the LORD.

(Numbers 28:17)
And in the fifteenth day of this month is the feast: seven days shall unleavened bread be eaten.

(Numbers 28:18)
In the first day shall be an holy convocation; you shall do no manner of servile work therein:

(Numbers 28:19)
But you shall offer a sacrifice made by fire for a burnt offering to the LORD; two young bullocks, and one ram, and seven lambs of the first year: they shall be to you without blemish:

(Numbers 28:20)
And their meat offering shall be of flour mingled with oil: three tenth deals shall you offer for a bullock, and two tenth deals for a ram;

(Numbers 28:21)
A several tenth deal shall you offer for every lamb, throughout the seven lambs:

(Numbers 28:22)
And one goat for a sin offering, to make an atonement for you.

(Numbers 28:23)
You shall offer these beside the burnt offering in the morning, which is for a continual burnt offering.

(Numbers 28:24)
After this manner you shall offer daily, throughout the seven days, the meat of the sacrifice made by fire, of a sweet savor to the LORD: it shall be offered beside the continual burnt offering, and his drink offering.

(Numbers 28:25)
And on the seventh day you shall have an holy convocation; you shall do no servile work.

(Numbers 28:26)
Also in the day of the firstfruits, when you bring a new meat offering to the LORD, after your weeks be out, you shall have an holy convocation; you shall do no servile work:

(Numbers 28:27)
But you shall offer the burnt offering for a sweet savor to the LORD; two young bullocks, one ram, seven lambs of the first year;

(Numbers 28:28)
And their meat offering of flour mingled with oil, three tenth deals to one bullock, two tenth deals to one ram,

(Numbers 28:29)
A several tenth deal to one lamb, throughout the seven lambs;

(Numbers 28:30)

And one kid of the goats, to make an atonement for you.

(Numbers 28:31)

You shall offer them beside the continual burnt offering, and his meat offering, (they shall be to you without blemish) and their drink offerings.

Numbers: Chapter Twenty-Nine

(Numbers 29:1)
And in the seventh month, on the first day of the month, you shall have an holy convocation; you shall do no servile work: it is a day of blowing the trumpets to you.

(Numbers 29:2)
And you shall offer a burnt offering for a sweet savor to the LORD; one young bullock, one ram, and seven lambs of the first year without blemish:

(Numbers 29:3)
And their meat offering shall be of flour mingled with oil, three tenth deals for a bullock, and two tenth deals for a ram,

(Numbers 29:4)
And one tenth deal for one lamb, throughout the seven lambs:

(Numbers 29:5)
And one kid of the goats for a sin offering, to make an atonement for you:

(Numbers 29:6)
Beside the burnt offering of the month, and his meat offering, and the daily burnt offering, and his meat offering, and their drink offerings, according to their manner, for a sweet savor, a sacrifice made by fire to the LORD.

(Numbers 29:7)
And you shall have on the tenth day of this seventh month an

holy convocation; and you shall afflict your souls: you shall not do any work therein:

(Numbers 29:8)

But you shall offer a burnt offering to the LORD for a sweet savor; one young bullock, one ram, and seven lambs of the first year; they shall be to you without blemish:

(Numbers 29:9)

And their meat offering shall be of flour mingled with oil, three tenth deals to a bullock, and two tenth deals to one ram,

(Numbers 29:10)

A several tenth deal for one lamb, throughout the seven lambs:

(Numbers 29:11)

One kid of the goats for a sin offering; beside the sin offering of atonement, and the continual burnt offering, and the meat offering of it, and their drink offerings.

(Numbers 29:12)

And on the fifteenth day of the seventh month you shall have an holy convocation; you shall do no servile work, and you shall keep a feast to the LORD seven days:

(Numbers 29:13)

And you shall offer a burnt offering, a sacrifice made by fire, of a sweet savor to the LORD; thirteen young bullocks, two rams, and fourteen lambs of the first year; they shall be without blemish:

(Numbers 29:14)

And their meat offering shall be of flour mingled with oil,

three tenth deals to every bullock of the thirteen bullocks, two tenth deals to each ram of the two rams,

(Numbers 29:15)
And a several tenth deal to each lamb of the fourteen lambs:

(Numbers 29:16)
And one kid of the goats for a sin offering; beside the continual burnt offering, his meat offering, and his drink offering.

(Numbers 29:17)
And on the second day you shall offer twelve young bullocks, two rams, fourteen lambs of the first year without spot:

(Numbers 29:18)
And their meat offering and their drink offerings for the bullocks, for the rams, and for the lambs, shall be according to their number, after the manner:

(Numbers 29:19)
And one kid of the goats for a sin offering; beside the continual burnt offering, and the meat offering thereof, and their drink offerings.

(Numbers 29:20)
And on the third day eleven bullocks, two rams, fourteen lambs of the first year without blemish;

(Numbers 29:21)
And their meat offering and their drink offerings for the bullocks, for the rams, and for the lambs, shall be according to their number, after the manner:

(Numbers 29:22)
And one goat for a sin offering; beside the continual burnt offering, and his meat offering, and his drink offering.

(Numbers 29:23)
And on the fourth day ten bullocks, two rams, and fourteen lambs of the first year without blemish:

(Numbers 29:24)
Their meat offering and their drink offerings for the bullocks, for the rams, and for the lambs, shall be according to their number, after the manner:

(Numbers 29:25)
And one kid of the goats for a sin offering; beside the continual burnt offering, his meat offering, and his drink offering.

(Numbers 29:26)
And on the fifth day nine bullocks, two rams, and fourteen lambs of the first year without spot:

(Numbers 29:27)
And their meat offering and their drink offerings for the bullocks, for the rams, and for the lambs, shall be according to their number, after the manner:

(Numbers 29:28)
And one goat for a sin offering; beside the continual burnt offering, and his meat offering, and his drink offering.

(Numbers 29:29)
And on the sixth day eight bullocks, two rams, and fourteen lambs of the first year without blemish:

(Numbers 29:30)

And their meat offering and their drink offerings for the bullocks, for the rams, and for the lambs, shall be according to their number, after the manner:

(Numbers 29:31)

And one goat for a sin offering; beside the continual burnt offering, his meat offering, and his drink offering.

(Numbers 29:32)

And on the seventh day seven bullocks, two rams, and fourteen lambs of the first year without blemish:

(Numbers 29:33)

And their meat offering and their drink offerings for the bullocks, for the rams, and for the lambs, shall be according to their number, after the manner:

(Numbers 29:34)

And one goat for a sin offering; beside the continual burnt offering, his meat offering, and his drink offering.

(Numbers 29:35)

On the eighth day you shall have a solemn assembly: you shall do no servile work therein:

(Numbers 29:36)

But you shall offer a burnt offering, a sacrifice made by fire, of a sweet savor to the LORD: one bullock, one ram, seven lambs of the first year without blemish:

(Numbers 29:37)

Their meat offering and their drink offerings for the bullock, for the ram, and for the lambs, shall be according to their number, after the manner:

(Numbers 29:38)

And one goat for a sin offering; beside the continual burnt offering, and his meat offering, and his drink offering.

(Numbers 29:39)

These things you shall do to the LORD in your set feasts, beside your vows, and your freewill offerings, for your burnt offerings, and for your meat offerings, and for your drink offerings, and for your peace offerings.

(Numbers 29:40)

And Moses told the children of Israel according to all that the LORD commanded Moses.

Numbers: Chapter Thirty

(Numbers 30:1)

And Moses spoke to the heads of the tribes concerning the children of Israel, saying, This is the thing which the LORD has commanded.

(Numbers 30:2)

If a man vow a vow to the LORD, or swear an oath to bind his soul with a bond; he shall not break his word, he shall do according to all that proceeds out of his mouth.

(Numbers 30:3)

If a woman also vow a vow to the LORD, and bind herself by a bond, being in her father's house in her youth;

(Numbers 30:4)

And her father hear her vow, and her bond wherewith she has bound her soul, and her father shall hold his peace at her: then all her vows shall stand, and every bond wherewith she has bound her soul shall stand.

(Numbers 30:5)

But if her father disallow her in the day that he hears; not any of her vows, or of her bonds wherewith she has bound her soul, shall stand: and the LORD shall forgive her, because her father disallowed her.

(Numbers 30:6)

And if she had at all an husband, when she vowed, or uttered ought out of her lips, wherewith she bound her soul;

(Numbers 30:7)

And her husband heard it, and held his peace at her in the day that he heard it: then her vows shall stand, and her bonds wherewith she bound her soul shall stand.

(Numbers 30:8)

But if her husband disallowed her on the day that he heard it; then he shall make her vow which she vowed, and that which she uttered with her lips, wherewith she bound her soul, of none effect: and the LORD shall forgive her.

(Numbers 30:9)

But every vow of a widow, and of her that is divorced, wherewith they have bound their souls, shall stand against her.

(Numbers 30:10)

And if she vowed in her husband's house, or bound her soul by a bond with an oath;

(Numbers 30:11)

And her husband heard it, and held his peace at her, and disallowed her not: then all her vows shall stand, and every bond wherewith she bound her soul shall stand.

(Numbers 30:12)

But if her husband has utterly made them void on the day he heard them; then whatsoever proceeded out of her lips concerning her vows, or concerning the bond of her soul, shall not stand: her husband has made them void; and the LORD shall forgive her.

(Numbers 30:13)

Every vow, and every binding oath to afflict the soul, her

husband may establish it, or her husband may make it void.

(Numbers 30:14)

But if her husband altogether hold his peace at her from day to day; then he establishes all her vows, or all her bonds, which are upon her: he confirms them, because he held his peace at her in the day that he heard them.

(Numbers 30:15)

But if he shall any ways make them void after that he has heard them; then he shall bear her iniquity.

(Numbers 30:16)

These are the statutes, which the LORD commanded Moses, between a man and his wife, between the father and his daughter, being yet in her youth in her father's house.

Numbers: Chapter Thirty-One

(Numbers 31:1) (Jasher 86:6...)
And it was after this that the LORD spoke to Moses, saying,

(Numbers 31:2) (...Jasher 86:6)
Say to the children of Israel to avenge the cause of their brothers the children of Israel upon the Midianites: afterward shall you be gathered to your people.

(Numbers 31:3) (Jasher 86:7...)
And Moses did so, and Moses spoke to the people, saying, Arm some of yourselves to the war, and let them go against the Midianites, and avenge the LORD of Midian.

(Numbers 31:4)
Of every tribe a thousand, throughout all the tribes of Israel, shall you send to the war.

(...Jasher 86:7...)
And the children of Israel chose from among them twelve thousand men, being one thousand to a tribe.

(Numbers 31:5)
So there were delivered out of the thousands of Israel, a thousand of every tribe, twelve thousand armed for war.

(Numbers 31:6) (...Jasher 86:7)
And Moses sent them, and they went to Midian to the war, a thousand of every tribe, them and Phinehas the son of Eleazar the priest, to the war, with the holy instruments, and the

trumpets to blow in his hand.

(Numbers 31:7) (Jasher 86:8...)
And the children of Israel, they warred against the Midianites, as the LORD commanded Moses; and they slew all the males.

(Numbers 31:8) (...Jasher 86:8)
And they slew the kings of Midian, beside the rest of them that were slain; namely, Evi, and Rekem, and Zur, and Hur, and Reba, five kings of Midian: Balaam also the son of Beor they slew with the sword.

(Numbers 31:9) (Jasher 86:9)
And the children of Israel took all the women of Midian captives, and their little ones, and took the spoil of all their cattle, and all their flocks, and all their goods.

(Numbers 31:10)
And they burnt all their cities wherein they dwelt, and all their goodly castles, with fire.

(Numbers 31:11) (Jasher 86:10...)
And they took all the spoil, and all the prey, both of men and of beasts.

(Numbers 31:12) (...Jasher 86:10)
And they brought the captives, and the prey, and the spoil, to Moses, and Eleazar the priest, and to the congregation of the children of Israel, to the camp at the plains of Moab, which are by Jordan near Jericho.

(Numbers 31:13) (Jasher 86:11)
And Moses, and Eleazar the priest, and all the princes of the

congregation, went forth to meet them without the camp with joy.

(Numbers 31:14)

And Moses was wroth with the officers of the host, with the captains over thousands, and captains over hundreds, which came from the battle.

(Numbers 31:15)

And Moses said to them, Have you saved all the women alive?

(Numbers 31:16)

Behold, these caused the children of Israel, through the counsel of Balaam, to commit trespass against the LORD in the matter of Peor, and there was a plague among the congregation of the LORD.

(Numbers 31:17)

Now therefore kill every male among the little ones, and kill every woman that has known man by lying with him.

(Numbers 31:18)

But all the women children, that have not known a man by lying with him, keep alive for yourselves.

(Numbers 31:19)

And do you abide without the camp seven days: whosoever has killed any person, and whosoever has touched any slain, purify both yourselves and your captives on the third day, and on the seventh day.

(Numbers 31:20)

And purify all your raiment, and all that is made of skins, and all work of goats' hair, and all things made of wood.

(Numbers 31:21)
And Eleazar the priest said to the men of war which went to the battle, This is the ordinance of the law which the LORD commanded Moses;

(Numbers 31:22)
Only the gold, and the silver, the brass, the iron, the tin, and the lead,

(Numbers 31:23)
Every thing that may abide the fire, you shall make it go through the fire, and it shall be clean: nevertheless it shall be purified with the water of separation: and all that abides not the fire you shall make go through the water.

(Numbers 31:24)
And you shall wash your clothes on the seventh day, and you shall be clean, and afterward you shall come into the camp.

(Numbers 31:25)
And the LORD spoke to Moses, saying,

(Numbers 31:26)
Take the sum of the prey that was taken, both of man and of beast, you, and Eleazar the priest, and the chief fathers of the congregation:

(Numbers 31:27)
And divide the prey into two parts; between them that took the war upon them, who went out to battle, and between all the congregation:

(Numbers 31:28)
And levy a tribute to the LORD of the men of war which went

out to battle: one soul of five hundred, both of the persons, and of the beeves, and of the donkeys, and of the sheep:

(Numbers 31:29)
Take it of their half, and give it to Eleazar the priest, for an heave offering of the LORD.

(Numbers 31:30)
And of the children of Israel's half, you shall take one portion of fifty, of the persons, of the beeves, of the donkeys, and of the flocks, of all manner of beasts, and give them to the Levites, which keep the charge of the tabernacle of the LORD.

(Numbers 31:31) (Jasher 86:12...)
And Moses and Eleazar the priest did as the LORD commanded Moses, and they divided the spoil of Midian.

(Numbers 31:32)
And the booty, being the rest of the prey which the men of war had caught, was six hundred thousand and seventy thousand and five thousand sheep,

(Numbers 31:33)
And threescore and twelve thousand beeves,

(Numbers 31:34)
And threescore and one thousand donkeys,

(Numbers 31:35)
And thirty and two thousand persons in all, of women that had not known man by lying with him.

(Numbers 31:36)
And the half, which was the portion of them that went out to

war, was in number three hundred thousand and seven and thirty thousand and five hundred sheep:

(Numbers 31:37)
And the LORD'S tribute of the sheep was six hundred and threescore and fifteen.

(Numbers 31:38)
And the beeves were thirty and six thousand; of which the LORD'S tribute was threescore and twelve.

(Numbers 31:39)
And the donkeys were thirty thousand and five hundred; of which the LORD'S tribute was threescore and one.

(Numbers 31:40)
And the persons were sixteen thousand; of which the LORD'S tribute was thirty and two persons.

(Numbers 31:41)
And Moses gave the tribute, which was the LORD'S heave offering, to Eleazar the priest, as the LORD commanded Moses.

(Numbers 31:42)
And of the children of Israel's half, which Moses divided from the men that warred,

(Numbers 31:43)
(Now the half that pertained to the congregation was three hundred thousand and thirty thousand and seven thousand and five hundred sheep,

(Numbers 31:44)

And thirty and six thousand beeves,

(Numbers 31:45)

And thirty thousand donkeys and five hundred,

(Numbers 31:46)

And sixteen thousand persons;)

(Numbers 31:47)

Even of the children of Israel's half, Moses took one portion of fifty, both of man and of beast, and gave them to the Levites, which kept the charge of the tabernacle of the LORD; as the LORD commanded Moses.

(Numbers 31:48)

And the officers which were over thousands of the host, the captains of thousands, and captains of hundreds, came near to Moses:

(Numbers 31:49)

And they said to Moses, Your servants have taken the sum of the men of war which are under our charge, and there lacks not one man of us.

(Numbers 31:50)

We have therefore brought an oblation for the LORD, what every man has gotten, of jewels of gold, chains, and bracelets, rings, earrings, and tablets, to make an atonement for our souls before the LORD.

(Numbers 31:51)

And Moses and Eleazar the priest took the gold of them, even all wrought jewels.

(Numbers 31:52)

And all the gold of the offering that they offered up to the LORD, of the captains of thousands, and of the captains of hundreds, was sixteen thousand seven hundred and fifty shekels.

(Numbers 31:53)

(For the men of war had taken spoil, every man for himself.)

(Numbers 31:54)

And Moses and Eleazar the priest took the gold of the captains of thousands and of hundreds, and brought it into the tabernacle of the congregation, for a memorial for the children of Israel before the LORD.

(...Jasher 86:12)

And the children of Israel had been revenged upon Midian for the cause of their brothers the children of Israel.

Numbers: Chapter Thirty-Two

(Numbers 32:1)

Now the children of Reuben and the children of Gad had a very great multitude of cattle: and when they saw the land of Jazer, and the land of Gilead, that, behold, the place was a place for cattle;

(Numbers 32:2)

The children of Gad and the children of Reuben came and spoke to Moses, and to Eleazar the priest, and to the princes of the congregation, saying,

(Numbers 32:3)

Ataroth, and Dibon, and Jazer, and Nimrah, and Heshbon, and Elealeh, and Shebam, and Nebo, and Beon,

(Numbers 32:4)

Even the country which the LORD smote before the congregation of Israel, is a land for cattle, and your servants have cattle:

(Numbers 32:5)

Why, said they, if we have found grace in your sight, let this land be given to your servants for a possession, and bring us not over Jordan.

(Numbers 32:6)

And Moses said to the children of Gad and to the children of Reuben, Shall your brethren go to war, and shall you sit here?

(Numbers 32:7)

And why discourage you the heart of the children of Israel from going over into the land which the LORD has given them?

(Numbers 32:8)

Thus did your fathers, when I sent them from Kadeshbarnea to see the land.

(Numbers 32:9)

For when they went up to the valley of Eshcol, and saw the land, they discouraged the heart of the children of Israel, that they should not go into the land which the LORD had given them.

(Numbers 32:10)

And the LORD'S anger was kindled the same time, and he swore, saying,

(Numbers 32:11)

Surely none of the men that came up out of Egypt, from twenty years old and upward, shall see the land which I swore to Abraham, to Isaac, and to Jacob; because they have not wholly followed me:

(Numbers 32:12)

Save Caleb the son of Jephunneh the Kenezite, and Joshua the son of Nun: for they have wholly followed the LORD.

(Numbers 32:13)

And the LORD'S anger was kindled against Israel, and he made them wander in the wilderness forty years, until all the generation, that had done evil in the sight of the LORD, was consumed.

(Numbers 32:14)

And, behold, you are risen up in your fathers' stead, an increase of sinful men, to augment yet the fierce anger of the LORD toward Israel.

(Numbers 32:15)

For if you turn away from after him, he will yet again leave them in the wilderness; and you shall destroy all this people.

(Numbers 32:16)

And they came near to him, and said, We will build sheepfolds here for our cattle, and cities for our little ones:

(Numbers 32:17)

But we ourselves will go ready armed before the children of Israel, until we have brought them to their place: and our little ones shall dwell in the fenced cities because of the inhabitants of the land.

(Numbers 32:18)

We will not return to our houses, until the children of Israel have inherited every man his inheritance.

(Numbers 32:19)

For we will not inherit with them on yonder side Jordan, or forward; because our inheritance is fallen to us on this side Jordan eastward.

(Numbers 32:20)

And Moses said to them, If you will do this thing, if you will go armed before the LORD to war,

(Numbers 32:21)

And will go all of you armed over Jordan before the LORD,

until he has driven out his enemies from before him,

(Numbers 32:22)
And the land be subdued before the LORD: then afterward you shall return, and be guiltless before the LORD, and before Israel; and this land shall be your possession before the LORD.

(Numbers 32:23)
But if you will not do so, behold, you have sinned against the LORD: and be sure your sin will find you out.

(Numbers 32:24)
Build you cities for your little ones, and folds for your sheep; and do that which has proceeded out of your mouth.

(Numbers 32:25)
And the children of Gad and the children of Reuben spoke to Moses, saying, Your servants will do as my lord commands.

(Numbers 32:26)
Our little ones, our wives, our flocks, and all our cattle, shall be there in the cities of Gilead:

(Numbers 32:27)
But your servants will pass over, every man armed for war, before the LORD to battle, as my lord says.

(Numbers 32:28)
So concerning them Moses commanded Eleazar the priest, and Joshua the son of Nun, and the chief fathers of the tribes of the children of Israel:

(Numbers 32:29)
And Moses said to them, If the children of Gad and the children

of Reuben will pass with you over Jordan, every man armed to battle, before the LORD, and the land shall be subdued before you; then you shall give them the land of Gilead for a possession:

(Numbers 32:30)

But if they will not pass over with you armed, they shall have possessions among you in the land of Canaan.

(Numbers 32:31)

And the children of Gad and the children of Reuben answered, saying, As the LORD has said to your servants, so will we do.

(Numbers 32:32)

We will pass over armed before the LORD into the land of Canaan, that the possession of our inheritance on this side Jordan may be ours.

(Numbers 32:33)

And Moses gave to them, even to the children of Gad, and to the children of Reuben, and to half the tribe of Manasseh the son of Joseph, the kingdom of Sihon king of the Amorites, and the kingdom of Og king of Bashan, the land, with the cities thereof in the coasts, even the cities of the country round about.

(Numbers 32:34)

And the children of Gad built Dibon, and Ataroth, and Aroer,

(Numbers 32:35)

And Atroth, Shophan, and Jaazer, and Jogbehah,

(Numbers 32:36)

And Bethnimrah, and Bethharan, fenced cities: and folds for sheep.

(Numbers 32:37)

And the children of Reuben built Heshbon, and Elealeh, and Kirjathaim,

(Numbers 32:38)

And Nebo, and Baalmeon, (their names being changed,) and Shibmah: and gave other names to the cities which they builded.

(Numbers 32:39)

And the children of Machir the son of Manasseh went to Gilead, and took it, and dispossessed the Amorite which was in it.

(Numbers 32:40)

And Moses gave Gilead to Machir the son of Manasseh; and he dwelt therein.

(Numbers 32:41)

And Jair the son of Manasseh went and took the small towns thereof, and called them Havothjair.

(Numbers 32:42)

And Nobah went and took Kenath, and the villages thereof, and called it Nobah, after his own name.

Numbers: Chapter Thirty-Three

(Numbers 33:1)

These are the journeys of the children of Israel, which went forth out of the land of Egypt with their armies under the hand of Moses and Aaron.

(Numbers 33:2)

And Moses wrote their goings out according to their journeys by the commandment of the LORD: and these are their journeys according to their goings out.

(Numbers 33:3)

And they departed from Rameses in the first month, on the fifteenth day of the first month; on the morrow after the passover the children of Israel went out with an high hand in the sight of all the Egyptians.

(Numbers 33:4)

For the Egyptians buried all their firstborn, which the LORD had smitten among them: upon their gods also the LORD executed judgments.

(Numbers 33:5)

And the children of Israel removed from Rameses, and pitched in Succoth.

(Numbers 33:6)

And they departed from Succoth, and pitched in Etham, which is in the edge of the wilderness.

(Numbers 33:7)

And they removed from Etham, and turned again to Pihahiroth, which is before Baalzephon: and they pitched before Migdol.

(Numbers 33:8)

And they departed from before Pihahiroth, and passed through the midst of the sea into the wilderness, and went three days' journey in the wilderness of Etham, and pitched in Marah.

(Numbers 33:9)

And they removed from Marah, and came to Elim: and in Elim were twelve fountains of water, and threescore and ten palm trees; and they pitched there.

(Numbers 33:10)

And they removed from Elim, and encamped by the Red sea.

(Numbers 33:11)

And they removed from the Red sea, and encamped in the wilderness of Sin.

(Numbers 33:12)

And they took their journey out of the wilderness of Sin, and encamped in Dophkah.

(Numbers 33:13)

And they departed from Dophkah, and encamped in Alush.

(Numbers 33:14)

And they removed from Alush, and encamped at Rephidim, where was no water for the people to drink.

(Numbers 33:15)

And they departed from Rephidim, and pitched in the wilderness of Sinai.

(Numbers 33:16)

And they removed from the desert of Sinai, and pitched at Kibrothhattaavah.

(Numbers 33:17)

And they departed from Kibrothhattaavah, and encamped at Hazeroth.

(Numbers 33:18)

And they departed from Hazeroth, and pitched in Rithmah.

(Numbers 33:19)

And they departed from Rithmah, and pitched at Rimmonparez.

(Numbers 33:20)

And they departed from Rimmonparez, and pitched in Libnah.

(Numbers 33:21)

And they removed from Libnah, and pitched at Rissah.

(Numbers 33:22)

And they journeyed from Rissah, and pitched in Kehelathah.

(Numbers 33:23)

And they went from Kehelathah, and pitched in mount Shapher.

(Numbers 33:24)
And they removed from mount Shapher, and encamped in Haradah.

(Numbers 33:25)
And they removed from Haradah, and pitched in Makheloth.

(Numbers 33:26)
And they removed from Makheloth, and encamped at Tahath.

(Numbers 33:27)
And they departed from Tahath, and pitched at Tarah.

(Numbers 33:28)
And they removed from Tarah, and pitched in Mithcah.

(Numbers 33:29)
And they went from Mithcah, and pitched in Hashmonah.

(Numbers 33:30)
And they departed from Hashmonah, and encamped at Moseroth.

(Numbers 33:31)
And they departed from Moseroth, and pitched in Benejaakan.

(Numbers 33:32)
And they removed from Benejaakan, and encamped at Horhagidgad.

(Numbers 33:33)
And they went from Horhagidgad, and pitched in Jotbathah.

(Numbers 33:34)
And they removed from Jotbathah, and encamped at Ebronah.

(Numbers 33:35)
And they departed from Ebronah, and encamped at Eziongaber.

(Numbers 33:36)
And they removed from Eziongaber, and pitched in the wilderness of Zin, which is Kadesh.

(Numbers 33:37)
And they removed from Kadesh, and pitched in mount Hor, in the edge of the land of Edom.

(Numbers 33:38)
And Aaron the priest went up into mount Hor at the commandment of the LORD, and died there, in the fortieth year after the children of Israel were come out of the land of Egypt, in the first day of the fifth month.

(Numbers 33:39)
And Aaron was an hundred and twenty and three years old when he died in mount Hor.

(Numbers 33:40)
And king Arad the Canaanite, which dwelt in the south in the land of Canaan, heard of the coming of the children of Israel.

(Numbers 33:41)
And they departed from mount Hor, and pitched in Zalmonah.

(Numbers 33:42)
And they departed from Zalmonah, and pitched in Punon.

(Numbers 33:43)
And they departed from Punon, and pitched in Oboth.

(Numbers 33:44)
And they departed from Oboth, and pitched in Ijeabarim, in the border of Moab.

(Numbers 33:45)
And they departed from Iim, and pitched in Dibongad.

(Numbers 33:46)
And they removed from Dibongad, and encamped in Almondiblathaim.

(Numbers 33:47)
And they removed from Almondiblathaim, and pitched in the mountains of Abarim, before Nebo.

(Numbers 33:48)
And they departed from the mountains of Abarim, and pitched in the plains of Moab by Jordan near Jericho.

(Numbers 33:49)
And they pitched by Jordan, from Bethjesimoth even to Abelshittim in the plains of Moab.

(Numbers 33:50)
And the LORD spoke to Moses in the plains of Moab by Jordan near Jericho, saying,

(Numbers 33:51)
Speak to the children of Israel, and say to them, When you are passed over Jordan into the land of Canaan;

(Numbers 33:52)
Then you shall drive out all the inhabitants of the land from before you, and destroy all their pictures, and destroy all their molten images, and quite pluck down all their high places:

(Numbers 33:53)
And you shall dispossess the inhabitants of the land, and dwell therein: for I have given you the land to possess it.

(Numbers 33:54)
And you shall divide the land by lot for an inheritance among your families: and to the more you shall give the more inheritance, and to the fewer you shall give the less inheritance: every man's inheritance shall be in the place where his lot falls; according to the tribes of your fathers you shall inherit.

(Numbers 33:55)
But if you will not drive out the inhabitants of the land from before you; then it shall come to pass, that those which you let remain of them shall be pricks in your eyes, and thorns in your sides, and shall vex you in the land wherein you dwell.

(Numbers 33:56)
Moreover it shall come to pass, that I shall do to you, as I thought to do to them.

Numbers: Chapter Thirty-Four

(Numbers 34:1)
And the LORD spoke to Moses, saying,

(Numbers 34:2)
Command the children of Israel, and say to them, When you come into the land of Canaan; (this is the land that shall fall to you for an inheritance, even the land of Canaan with the coasts thereof:)

(Numbers 34:3)
Then your south quarter shall be from the wilderness of Zin along by the coast of Edom, and your south border shall be the outermost coast of the salt sea eastward:

(Numbers 34:4)
And your border shall turn from the south to the ascent of Akrabbim, and pass on to Zin: and the going forth thereof shall be from the south to Kadeshbarnea, and shall go on to Hazaraddar, and pass on to Azmon:

(Numbers 34:5)
And the border shall fetch a compass from Azmon to the river of Egypt, and the goings out of it shall be at the sea.

(Numbers 34:6)
And as for the western border, you shall even have the great sea for a border: this shall be your west border.

(Numbers 34:7)
And this shall be your north border: from the great sea you shall point out for you mount Hor:

(Numbers 34:8)
From mount Hor you shall point out your border to the entrance of Hamath; and the goings forth of the border shall be to Zedad:

(Numbers 34:9)
And the border shall go on to Ziphron, and the goings out of it shall be at Hazarenan: this shall be your north border.

(Numbers 34:10)
And you shall point out your east border from Hazarenan to Shepham:

(Numbers 34:11)
And the coast shall go down from Shepham to Riblah, on the east side of Ain; and the border shall descend, and shall reach to the side of the sea of Chinnereth eastward:

(Numbers 34:12)
And the border shall go down to Jordan, and the goings out of it shall be at the salt sea: this shall be your land with the coasts thereof round about.

(Numbers 34:13)
And Moses commanded the children of Israel, saying, This is the land which you shall inherit by lot, which the LORD commanded to give to the nine tribes, and to the half tribe:

(Numbers 34:14)
For the tribe of the children of Reuben according to the house

of their fathers, and the tribe of the children of Gad according to the house of their fathers, have received their inheritance; and half the tribe of Manasseh have received their inheritance:

(Numbers 34:15)
The two tribes and the half tribe have received their inheritance on this side Jordan near Jericho eastward, toward the sunrising.

(Numbers 34:16)
And the LORD spoke to Moses, saying,

(Numbers 34:17)
These are the names of the men which shall divide the land to you: Eleazar the priest, and Joshua the son of Nun.

(Numbers 34:18)
And you shall take one prince of every tribe, to divide the land by inheritance.

(Numbers 34:19)
And the names of the men are these: Of the tribe of Judah, Caleb the son of Jephunneh.

(Numbers 34:20)
And of the tribe of the children of Simeon, Shemuel the son of Ammihud.

(Numbers 34:21)
Of the tribe of Benjamin, Elidad the son of Chislon.

(Numbers 34:22)
And the prince of the tribe of the children of Dan, Bukki the son of Jogli.

(Numbers 34:23)

The prince of the children of Joseph, for the tribe of the children of Manasseh, Hanniel the son of Ephod.

(Numbers 34:24)

And the prince of the tribe of the children of Ephraim, Kemuel the son of Shiphtan.

(Numbers 34:25)

And the prince of the tribe of the children of Zebulun, Elizaphan the son of Parnach.

(Numbers 34:26)

And the prince of the tribe of the children of Issachar, Paltiel the son of Azzan.

(Numbers 34:27)

And the prince of the tribe of the children of Asher, Ahihud the son of Shelomi.

(Numbers 34:28)

And the prince of the tribe of the children of Naphtali, Pedahel the son of Ammihud.

(Numbers 34:29)

These are they whom the LORD commanded to divide the inheritance to the children of Israel in the land of Canaan.

Numbers: Chapter Thirty-Five

(Numbers 35:1)
And the LORD spoke to Moses in the plains of Moab by Jordan near Jericho, saying,

(Numbers 35:2)
Command the children of Israel, that they give to the Levites of the inheritance of their possession cities to dwell in; and you shall give also to the Levites suburbs for the cities round about them.

(Numbers 35:3)
And the cities shall they have to dwell in; and the suburbs of them shall be for their cattle, and for their goods, and for all their beasts.

(Numbers 35:4)
And the suburbs of the cities, which you shall give to the Levites, shall reach from the wall of the city and outward a thousand cubits round about.

(Numbers 35:5)
And you shall measure from without the city on the east side two thousand cubits, and on the south side two thousand cubits, and on the west side two thousand cubits, and on the north side two thousand cubits; and the city shall be in the midst: this shall be to them the suburbs of the cities.

(Numbers 35:6)
And among the cities which you shall give to the Levites there

shall be six cities for refuge, which you shall appoint for the manslayer, that he may flee there: and to them you shall add forty and two cities.

(Numbers 35:7)
So all the cities which you shall give to the Levites shall be forty and eight cities: them shall you give with their suburbs.

(Numbers 35:8)
And the cities which you shall give shall be of the possession of the children of Israel: from them that have many you shall give many; but from them that have few you shall give few: every one shall give of his cities to the Levites according to his inheritance which he inherits.

(Numbers 35:9)
And the LORD spoke to Moses, saying,

(Numbers 35:10)
Speak to the children of Israel, and say to them, When you be come over Jordan into the land of Canaan;

(Numbers 35:11)
Then you shall appoint you cities to be cities of refuge for you; that the slayer may flee there, which kills any person at unawares.

(Numbers 35:12)
And they shall be to you cities for refuge from the avenger; that the manslayer die not, until he stand before the congregation in judgment.

(Numbers 35:13)
And of these cities which you shall give six cities shall you

have for refuge.

(Numbers 35:14)

You shall give three cities on this side Jordan, and three cities shall you give in the land of Canaan, which shall be cities of refuge.

(Numbers 35:15)

These six cities shall be a refuge, both for the children of Israel, and for the stranger, and for the sojourner among them: that every one that kills any person unawares may flee there.

(Numbers 35:16)

And if he smite him with an instrument of iron, so that he die, he is a murderer: the murderer shall surely be put to death.

(Numbers 35:17)

And if he smite him with throwing a stone, wherewith he may die, and he die, he is a murderer: the murderer shall surely be put to death.

(Numbers 35:18)

Or if he smite him with an hand weapon of wood, wherewith he may die, and he die, he is a murderer: the murderer shall surely be put to death.

(Numbers 35:19)

The revenger of blood himself shall slay the murderer: when he meets him, he shall slay him.

(Numbers 35:20)

But if he thrust him of hatred, or hurl at him by laying of wait, that he die;

(Numbers 35:21)

Or in enmity smite him with his hand, that he die: he that smote him shall surely be put to death; for he is a murderer: the revenger of blood shall slay the murderer, when he meets him.

(Numbers 35:22)

But if he thrust him suddenly without enmity, or have cast upon him any thing without laying of wait,

(Numbers 35:23)

Or with any stone, wherewith a man may die, seeing him not, and cast it upon him, that he die, and was not his enemy, neither sought his harm:

(Numbers 35:24)

Then the congregation shall judge between the slayer and the revenger of blood according to these judgments:

(Numbers 35:25)

And the congregation shall deliver the slayer out of the hand of the revenger of blood, and the congregation shall restore him to the city of his refuge, whither he was fled: and he shall abide in it to the death of the high priest, which was anointed with the holy oil.

(Numbers 35:26)

But if the slayer shall at any time come without the border of the city of his refuge, whither he was fled;

(Numbers 35:27)

And the revenger of blood find him without the borders of the city of his refuge, and the revenger of blood kill the slayer; he shall not be guilty of blood:

(Numbers 35:28)

Because he should have remained in the city of his refuge until the death of the high priest: but after the death of the high priest the slayer shall return into the land of his possession.

(Numbers 35:29)

So these things shall be for a statute of judgment to you throughout your generations in all your dwellings.

(Numbers 35:30)

Whoso kills any person, the murderer shall be put to death by the mouth of witnesses: but one witness shall not testify against any person to cause him to die.

(Numbers 35:31)

Moreover you shall take no satisfaction for the life of a murderer, which is guilty of death: but he shall be surely put to death.

(Numbers 35:32)

And you shall take no satisfaction for him that is fled to the city of his refuge, that he should come again to dwell in the land, until the death of the priest.

(Numbers 35:33)

So you shall not pollute the land wherein you are: for blood it defiles the land: and the land cannot be cleansed of the blood that is shed therein, but by the blood of him that shed it.

(Numbers 35:34)

Defile not therefore the land which you shall inhabit, wherein I dwell: for I the LORD dwell among the children of Israel.

Numbers: Chapter Thirty-Six

(Numbers 36:1)

And the chief fathers of the families of the children of Gilead, the son of Machir, the son of Manasseh, of the families of the sons of Joseph, came near, and spoke before Moses, and before the princes, the chief fathers of the children of Israel:

(Numbers 36:2)

And they said, The LORD commanded my lord to give the land for an inheritance by lot to the children of Israel: and my lord was commanded by the LORD to give the inheritance of Zelophehad our brother to his daughters.

(Numbers 36:3)

And if they are married to any of the sons of the other tribes of the children of Israel, then shall their inheritance be taken from the inheritance of our fathers, and shall be put to the inheritance of the tribe where they are received: so shall it be taken from the lot of our inheritance.

(Numbers 36:4)

And when the jubilee of the children of Israel shall be, then shall their inheritance be put to the inheritance of the tribe where they are received: so shall their inheritance be taken away from the inheritance of the tribe of our fathers.

(Numbers 36:5)

And Moses commanded the children of Israel according to the word of the LORD, saying, The tribe of the sons of Joseph has said well.

(Numbers 36:6)
This is the thing which the LORD do command concerning the daughters of Zelophehad, saying, Let them marry to whom they think best; only to the family of the tribe of their father shall they marry.

(Numbers 36:7)
So shall not the inheritance of the children of Israel remove from tribe to tribe: for every one of the children of Israel shall keep himself to the inheritance of the tribe of his fathers.

(Numbers 36:8)
And every daughter, that possesses an inheritance in any tribe of the children of Israel, shall be wife to one of the family of the tribe of her father, that the children of Israel may enjoy every man the inheritance of his fathers.

(Numbers 36:9)
Neither shall the inheritance remove from one tribe to another tribe; but every one of the tribes of the children of Israel shall keep himself to his own inheritance.

(Numbers 36:10)
Even as the LORD commanded Moses, so did the daughters of Zelophehad:

(Numbers 36:11)
For Mahlah, Tirzah, and Hoglah, and Milcah, and Noah, the daughters of Zelophehad, were married to their father's brothers' sons:

(Numbers 36:12)
And they were married into the families of the sons of

Manasseh the son of Joseph, and their inheritance remained in the tribe of the family of their father.

(Numbers 36:13)

These are the commandments and the judgments, which the LORD commanded by the hand of Moses to the children of Israel in the plains of Moab by Jordan near Jericho.

Final Notes

We hope your journey is enriched and you are blessed through the production of the **Ancient Texts and the Bible** series!

Minister 2 Others would like to hear from you. If you have comments or questions concerning our materials, or if you find errors in our projects, misspellings, or formatting issues. We work hard to provide quality materials, however, sometimes things can squeak by unnoticed. Your feedback is truly appreciated.

We love producing helpful, innovative books and we are grateful for your support! If you have enjoyed this production, please consider writing a review and letting others know about our materials.

If you would like to be updated when we release new books and other materials, please sign up for our e-newsletter on our website.

Thanks!

Minister 2 Others

Minister2others.com

www.ingramcontent.com/pod-product-compliance
Lightning Source LLC
Chambersburg PA
CBHW071255190726
48292CB00007B/2539

* 9 7 8 1 9 4 7 7 5 1 2 7 9 *